HOOP HYSTERIA II

The College Basketball Trivia Quiz Book

By Brent Flanders
Jeff Sigler
Randy Towner
Doug Vance

ADDAX
PUBLISHING
GROUP

Published by Addax Publishing Group
Copyright © 1999 by Brent Flanders and Jeff Sigler
Edited by J. Nelson Elliott
Designed by Randy Breeden
Cover Design by Randy Breeden

Photos Courtesy: The University of Oklahoma, Western Kentucky University, Providence College, UCLA, Oklahoma State University, Kansas State University, The University of Kansas, United States Naval Academy, Gonzaga University

For information address:
Addax Publishing Group
8643 Hauser Drive, Suite 235, Lenexa, Kansas 66215

Library of Congress Cataloging-in-Publication Data

Hoop hysteria II : the college basketball trivia quiz book / by Brent
Flanders ... [et al.].
        Continues: Hoop hysteria. c1997.
        ISBN 1-886110-62-X
        1. Basketball—United States—Miscellanea. I. Flanders,
        Brent E.
II. Hoop hysteria.
GV885.4.H66 1999
796.323'63'0973—dc21   98-24659
                                            CIP

DEDICATION

With special kudos to Dr. Naismith, we dedicate this book to all players and coaches, past and present, who have made college basketball what it is today.

Their participation in this fabulous game has produced an annual spectacle of sport that attracts millions. A late winter-early spring basketball bonanza known as March Madness.

It is our hope that the so-called trivia which is the subject of this book will serve as an archive of many memorable basketball seasons.

ENJOY!

Brent Flanders, Jeff Sigler, Randy Towner and Doug Vance

USING HOOP HYSTERIA
AS A GAME

In keeping with our original goal of creating a fun and exciting college basketball trivia game, we have designed this book to be played as a game!

Object of the Game - The object of the game is to score more points than your opponent!

Equipment - In addition to your *Hoop Hysteria* Trivia Book, you will need one common die, a wrist watch for a timer (optional), and a notepad and pencil (to keep score).

Beginning Play - Games are played between two teams. Teams may consist of one or more players. Teams decide before starting the game who is the home team and how the winner will be decided. Games can be played to a time limit or a preset point total, i.e., the first team to reach 100 points wins. Once these are established, a player on the visiting team tosses a coin and a player on the home team calls the toss. The winner of the coin toss is awarded possession of the die.

Playing the Game - The offense rolls the die to determine the play:

A roll of 1, 2, or 3 = Shot - If the die lands on a 1, 2, or 3, the offensive team gets the opportunity to answer a question. The defensive team opens the book randomly to a page and the offensive team chooses the question. If they answer correctly, they score the associated points. If they are incorrect, the die passes to their opponent.

A roll of 4 = Turnover - If the die lands on a 4, the offense loses possession and their opponent receives the die.

A roll of 5 = Defensive Foul - If the die lands on a 5, the

offensive team gets the opportunity to answer a question as above. If they are correct, they get the point total of the question plus an additional point. If they are incorrect, they continue to have possession of the die for the next play.

A roll of 6 = Offensive Foul - If the die lands on a 6, the

defensive team gets the opportunity to select the question for the offense. The defense opens the book randomly to a page and they choose a question. If the offense answers correctly the possession simply changes to the defensive team (it must have been a player-control foul!). If they answer incorrectly, the defense scores the points and receives possession of the die.

Game Format Tips - Certain rules should be decided prior to

beginning play. The following are some suggestions:

• Decide what constitutes a correct answer. For example, are both first and last names required to score points? You may decide to give one point for partially-correct answers. *Hoop Hysteria* questions are specific in what they are asking for; trivial tidbits provided with the answer are for educational purposes and are not intended to be a part of the answer.

• Decide how much time will be given to each team to answer a question. You may use a wrist watch or some other timing device to aid you.

• Choose one player to be the scorekeeper. Only this player should be allowed to change the score.

CONTENTS

GAME DIRECTIONS
Using *Hoop Hysteria* as a Game 4

CHAPTER 1
All-Americans...7

CHAPTER 2
Coaches..17

CHAPTER 3
I didn't know that 37

CHAPTER 4
Nicknames..45

CHAPTER 5
Places...59

CHAPTER 6
Players 71

CHAPTER 7
Records...99

CHAPTER 8
Tournaments..109

CHAPTER 1
ALL-AMERICANS

3-PT   **1** What Oregon State player was an All-American in 1981?

3-PT   **2** What Purdue forward was an All-American in 1961?

3-PT   **3** Don Goldstein, Darrell Griffith and John Turner were All-Americans at what university?

3-PT   **4** What 6-foot 9-inch Oklahoma player was a consensus All-American in 1983 and a unanimous All-American in 1984 and 1985?

3-PT   **5** Seton Hall has had two consensus All-Americans from 1940 through 1990. Name one of them.

3-PT   **6** Chris Jackson was a two-time All-American at what school?

3-PT   **7** What school did consensus All-American George Senesky compete for in 1943?

3-PT   **8** Who was Texas Western's first basketball All-American?

3-PT   **9** What Bradley player was an All-American in 1988?

3-PT   **10** Jeff Renick was the first two-time All-American at what Big 12 university?

3-PT   **11** Who played at UCLA, was a consensus All-American in 1976, and the MOP of the NCAA tournament in 1975?

2-PT   **12** Walt Williams became an All-American at the University of Maryland in 1992. Name three other All-Americans from Maryland.

1 Steve Johnson

2 Terry Dischinger

3 The University of Louisville

4 Wayman Tisdale

5 Bob Davies, in 1942, and Walt Dukes, in 1953

6 Louisiana State University

7 St. Joseph's, in Pennsylvannia

8 Jim Barnes

9 Hersey Hawkins

10 Oklahoma State

11 Rich Washington

12 John Lucas, Tom McMillan, Gene Shue, Buck Williams, Louis Berger, Len Bias, Len Elmore and Albert King

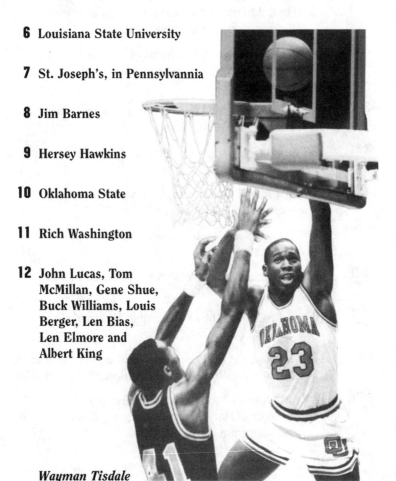

Wayman Tisdale

1-PT 13 What 7-foot 4-inch Virginia center was a unanimous first team All-American for three straight years from 1981 to 1983?

3-PT 14 Jules Bender and Irving Torgoff were unanimous All-Americans at what university in 1937 and 1939 respectively?

2-PT 15 Who was the first three-time All-American at Ohio State?

3-PT 16 What North Carolina forward was an All-American in 1972?

3-PT 17 At what school were Fred Pralle (1938), Howard Engleman (1941) and Charley Black (1943) consensus All-Americans?

2-PT 18 St. Bonaventure has produced two unanimous All-Americans. Name one of them.

3-PT 19 What team did consensus All-American Bob Lloyd compete for in 1967?

3-PT 20 Clem Haskins (1967) and Jim McDaniels (1971) were consensus All-Americans from what school?

3-PT 21 What Michigan player was an All-American in 1977?

3-PT 22 What Ohio State player was an All-American in 1964?

3-PT 23 What North Carolina player was an All-American in 1968?

2-PT 24 Who was the first three-time first team All-American to never appear in the NCAA tournament?

3-PT 25 What 6-foot 2-inch Cincinnati guard helped the Bearcats to NCAA titles in 1961 and 1962, and was a first team All-American in 1963?

3-PT 26 Murray Wier and Chuck Darling were All-Americans at what university in 1948 and 1952 respectively?

13 Ralph Sampson

14 Long Island University-Brooklyn

15 Jerry Lucas

16 Bob McAdoo

17 Kansas

18 Tom Stith, in 1961, and Bob Lanier, in 1970

19 Rutgers

20 Western Kentucky

21 Rickey Green, who was one of the first successful junior college players to make the jump to division one.

22 Gary Bradds

23 Larry Miller

24 Pete Maravich, of Louisiana State University

25 Tom Thacker

26 The University of Iowa

Clem Haskins

2-PT **27** Who was UNLV's first All-American?

3-PT **28** Jerry Harkness was a consensus All-American for what national championship team in 1963?

2-PT **29** Who was Iowa State's first All-American, selected in 1957? (Clue: He later became a sports announcer)

2-PT **30** What Minnesota Golden Gopher was a second team All-American in 1977, a first team All-American in 1978, and was from Nassau, Bahamas?

3-PT **31** What Duke player was an All-American in 1979?

3-PT **32** What Western Kentucky center was an All-American in 1971?

3-PT **33** What 6-foot 1-inch Rutgers guard earned All-American honors in 1967, while leading the nation in free throw percentage with a .921 mark?

3-PT **34** What Georgetown center was a consensus All-American in 1983 and a unanimous All-American in 1984 and 1985?

3-PT **35** What Davidson player was a unanimous All-American in 1965?

3-PT **36** Who was Louisville's first All-American?

3-PT **37** What 6-foot 9-inch Utah standout led the nation in scoring and earned first team All-American honors in 1962?

3-PT **38** For what school was Scott May an All-American in 1976?

3-PT **39** What NYU player was an All-American in 1963?

27 Ricky Sobers, in 1975

28 Loyola of Chicago

29 Gary Thompson

30 Mychal Thompson

31 Mike Gminski

32 Jim McDaniels

33 Bob Lloyd

34 Patrick Ewing

35 Fred Hetzel

36 Charlie Tyra, in 1955-56

37 Billy McGill

38 University of Indiana

39 Barry Kramer

Jim McDaniels

3-PT **40** What position did Clyde Lee, the All-American from Vanderbilt, play in college?

3-PT **41** What Kentucky guard was an All-American in 1980?

3-PT **42** What UCLA player was an All-American in 1971?

2-PT **43** For how many years was John Havlicek a consensus All-American at Ohio State?

3-PT **44** Tony Lavelli was the Player of the Year and consensus All-American in 1949 while playing for what Ivy League school?

3-PT **45** What Wichita State player was an All-American in 1964?

3-PT **46** What Providence player was an All-American in 1973?

3-PT **47** Rice had three consensus All-Americans from 1942 to 1945. Name one of them.

3-PT **48** What 6-foot 8-inch St. Louis University player was a unanimous first team All-American in 1949 while leading the nation in field goal percentage with a .524 mark?

3-PT **49** Charlie Tyra was a consensus All-American at what school in 1957?

3-PT **50** What Marquette guard was an All-American in 1971?

3-PT **51** What Houston player was an All-American in 1977? (Clue: Think of sparrow music)

3-PT **52** What Maryland player was an All-American in 1975?

3-PT **53** What Tennessee player was an All-American in 1983?

40   Center

41   Kyle Macy

42   Sidney Wicks

43   Zero

44   Yale

45   Dave Stallworth

46   Ernie DiGregorio

47   Bob Kinney, in 1942, Bill Closs, in
      1943, and Bill Henry, in 1945

48   Ed MaCauley

49   Louisville

50   Dean Meminger

51   Otis Birdsong

52   John Lucas,
      who was also an outstanding
      tennis player and future NBA
      player and coach.

53   Dale Ellis

Ernie DiGregorio

3-PT **54** What Purdue center was an All-American in 1980?

3-PT **55** Tom Chambers, Danny Vranes and Mike Newlin were All-Americans at what WAC university?

3-PT **56** What Vanderbilt player was a unanimous All-American in 1966?

3-PT **57** What 6-foot 8-inch SMU center averaged double-digit points and rebounds as a junior and a senior and was a first team All-American in 1957?

3-PT **58** For what college were Gus Broberg a unanimous All-American in 1941 and Audley Brindley a consensus All-American in 1944?

3-PT **59** What team did consensus All-American Tom Riker compete for in 1972?

3-PT **60** Bill Hapac, Andy Phillip, Walton Kirk and Rod Fletcher were consensus All-Americans from what Big 10 university?

2-PT **61** Who was DePaul's first All-American selection, earning the honor in 1944 and 1945?

3-PT **62** What Syracuse guard was an All-American in 1966?

3-PT **63** J. R. Reid was a consensus first team All-American in 1988 and a member of the Olympic team the same year. At what ACC school did J. R. Reid play?

3-PT **64** John "Cat" Thompson and Frank Ward were consensus All-Americans from what university in 1930?

3-PT **65** What DePaul player was an All-American in 1980?

3-PT **66** What 6-foot 11-inch Georgia player was an All-SEC performer in 1990, and an academic All-American in 1988, 1989 and 1990?

3-PT **67** What UCLA forward was an All-American in 1975?

54 Joe Barry Carroll

55 Utah

56 Clyde Lee

57 Jim Krebs

58 Dartmouth

59 South Carolina

60 Illinois

61 George Mikan

62 Dave Bing

63 The University of North Carolina

64 Montana State

65 Mark Aguirre

66 Alec Kessler

67 Dave Meyers

Dave Meyers

CHAPTER 2
COACHES

2-PT **1** What team has been led to the NCAA tournament by Fred Enke, Fred Snowden and Lute Olson?

3-PT **2** Who was the coach of the 1978-79 Indiana State team which lost in the NCAA final to Michigan State?

2-PT **3** What three teams has George Raveling guided to the NCAA tournament?

2-PT **4** Who coached Wilt Chamberlain at Kansas?

3-PT **5** What was the last school to beat a John Wooden-coached team?

2-PT **6** How many losing seasons did Dean Smith have at North Carolina?

2-PT **7** Frank McGuire, Joe Lapchick and Frank Mulzoff have all guided what team to the NCAA tournament?

2-PT **8** Who was named head coach at the University of Connecticut in May 1986?

3-PT **9** What coach was a backup center for Bill Russell in the NBA?

2-PT **10** What coach took his team to the 1989 NCAA national championship before ever winning a regular season game?

3-PT **11** Who was the last team to beat an Adolph Rupp-coached team?

2-PT **12** What coach led California to a 71-70 win over West Virginia for the 1959 NCAA title?

2-PT **13** Name two of the three teams that Frank McGuire has taken to the NCAA tournament.

1 Arizona

2 Bill Hodges

3 Washington State, Iowa and Southern Cal

4 Dick Harp

5 Washington beat UCLA 103-81 Feb. 22, 1975, following which, UCLA won the next eight games and the NCAA title.

6 One: his first team in 1962 of 8 wins, 9 losses.

7 St. John's

8 Jim Calhoun

9 John Thompson, of Georgetown

10 Steve Fisher, of Michigan

11 Florida State, in 1972

12 Pete Newell

13 St. John's, North Carolina and South Carolina

3-PT **14** Who became the first person to play for and coach an NIT championship team?

3-PT **15** Who was the most recent coach to lead two different teams to their schools' first appearance in the NCAA tournament?

3-PT **16** After 16 seasons as Virginia's coach, Terry Holland left to become athletic director of what university?

2-PT **17** Bill Lange and Ben Carnevale have both guided what team to the NCAA tournament?

2-PT **18** Who succeeded Ray Meyer as coach at DePaul?

2-PT **19** Where did Lefty Driesell attend college?

2-PT **20** How many NCAA tournaments did Lou Carnesecca take St. John's to?

2-PT **21** What team did later NBA coach Bill Fitch take to the NCAA tournament in 1968?

2-PT **22** Who succeeded John Wooden as coach at UCLA?

2-PT **23** Who won the NCAA title in only his sixth game as a head coach?

3-PT **24** Who was the first coach to guide four different schools to the NCAA tournament?

2-PT **25** Which Tennessee coach followed Darrell Griffith from high school to Louisville in 1978?

2-PT **26** What is Jerry Tarkanian's alma mater?

3-PT **27** NBA coaches Bill Sharman, Alex Hannum, Mack Calvin, Bob Kloppenburg, Tex Winter and Paul Westphal attended what university?

14 Jeff Jones, of Virginia

15 Matt Furjanic led Robert Morris, in 1982, and Marist, in 1986.

16 Davidson, which is his alma mater.

17 North Carolina

18 Joey Meyer, Ray's son

19 Duke University

20 Eighteen

21 Bowling Green

22 Gene Bartow

23 Steve Fisher, of Michigan, 1989

24 Eddie Sutton

25 Wade Houston

26 Fresno State

27 The University of Southern California

Gene Bartow

3-PT **28** Who was the first coach to take his alma mater to the NCAA title game after having played in the tournament as an undergraduate?

2-PT **29** Who succeeded Adolph Rupp as the coach at the University of Kentucky?

2-PT **30** Benny Dees and Tim Floyd have both taken what team to the NCAA tournament?

3-PT **31** Sox Walseth coached at what university from 1957-1976?

3-PT **32** Moe Iba, Gene Bartow and Dana Kirk all coached at what university?

2-PT **33** Who was the first coach to win back-to-back NCAA championships?

2-PT **34** What coach led Texas Western to a win over Kentucky for the 1966 NCAA title?

3-PT **35** Who is the first coach to win more than 25 NCAA tournament games yet never win the national championship?

2-PT **36** Who was Bob Knight's college coach at Ohio State?

3-PT **37** Name two Weber State coaches who went on to coach in the NBA.

2-PT **38** Name at least three of the six coaches who have coached in the NBA after winning NCAA championships.

3-PT **39** Who was the first major college coach to finish his career with more than 500 victories and never participate in the NCAA tournament?

3-PT **40** What former Wichita State coach took the Wheatshockers to their only appearance in The Final Four?

2-PT **41** Who served as head basketball coach at Notre Dame before Digger Phelp's appointment in 1971?

28 Don Donoher, of Dayton

29 Joe B. Hall

30 New Orleans

31 Colorado, which is bordered by no less that seven states (Wyoming, Nebraska, Kansas, Oklahoma, Utah, Arizona and New Mexico).

32 Memphis State

33 Henry Iba, of Oklahoma A&M, in 1945 and 1946

34 Don Haskins

35 Guy Lewis, of the University of Houston

36 Fred Taylor

37 Dick Motta and Phil Johnson

38 Larry Brown, Ed Jucker, Doggie Julian, Jerry Tarkanian, Rick Pitino and Frank McGuire

39 Glenn Wilkes, of Stetson

40 Gary Thompson

41 Johnny Dee

Henry Iba

42 From which ACC school did Charles "Lefty" Driesell graduate?

 43 Name two of the five coaches to have played and coached in a Final Four game.

 44 What nervous habit was UNLV head coach Jerry Tarkanian known for?

 45 What Kentucky standout from the mid sixties went on to enjoy an outstanding career as a NBA coach with the Lakers , Knicks and Heat?

 46 What Stanford coach had a perfect record in the NCAA tournament?

 47 From what school did Hall-of-Famer Arthur "Dutch" Lonborg graduate in 1921?

 48 What former San Francisco star became the first African-American coach in the NBA?

 49 Name two of the three teams Eddie Hickey has taken to the NCAA tournament.

 50 Which coach, as of 1997, had the most NCAA tournament appearances?

 51 Don Haskins, longtime coach at UTEP, played for what famous coach?

 52 What team was led to the NCAA tournament by C.M. Newton in 1975 and 1976?

 53 What former Villanova star and NBA coach is credited with the first three-point field goal in NBA history?

 54 Who were the first two coaches to lead two different schools to the NCAA title game?

 55 Who did Randy Ayers succeed as head basketball coach at Ohio State University?

56 P. J. Carlesimo, the former head coach at Seton Hall, attended what university?

42 Duke, in 1954

43 Vic Bubas, Dick Harp, Bob Knight, Bones McKinney and Dean Smith

44 Biting a towel during games

45 Pat Riley

46 Everett Dean, whose team was 3-0 in 1942 and won the title.

47 Kansas

48 Bill Russell

49 Creighton, St. Louis and Marquette

50 Dean Smith, of North Carolina, with 31 appearances

51 Henry Iba, of Oklahoma State

52 Alabama

53 Chris Ford made the first three-pointer on October 12, 1979.

54 Larry Brown and Frank McGuire

55 Gary Williams

56 Fordham

Larry Brown

2-PT **57** Eddie Fogler has taken which three teams to the NCAA tournament?

3-PT **58** Nolan Richardson attended what university?

2-PT **59** At what two schools did Hall of Fame inductee Jack Gardner coach during his 28 years as a Division I coach?

3-PT **60** What school has had coaches named Frosty, Bebe and Sox?

3-PT **61** Who played 11 years of pro ball, designed a basketball shoe in 1931, coached the Air Force basketball team in 1942, and conducted the first public basketball clinic?

3-PT **62** Georgia coach Hugh Durham played collegiately for what school?

2-PT **63** Who became the coach at Princeton in 1967?

2-PT **64** Larry Brown played collegiately at what ACC university?

3-PT **65** What three coaches have won an NCAA title, an NIT title and an Olympic gold medal?

3-PT **66** John Bach, Digger Phelps and Nick Macarchuk have all taken what school to the NCAA tournament?

2-PT **67** Who served as head coach at Oregon State for 36 years, winning 599 games, before retiring in 1964?

3-PT **68** Who coached Missouri in the 1989 NCAA tournament due to head coach Norm Stewart's illness?

3-PT **69** Who is credited with saying, "We have a great bunch of outside shooters. Unfortunately, all our games are played indoors?"

2-PT **70** How many undefeated seasons did John Wooden have while at UCLA?

57 Wichita State (1988), Vanderbilt (1991) and South Carolina (1998)

58 The University of Texas-El Paso

59 Kansas State and Utah

60 Colorado, with Frosty Cox, Bebe Lee and Sox Walseth

61 Charles (Chuck) Taylor

62 Florida State

63 Pete Carril

64 North Carolina

65 Bob Knight, Pete Newell and Dean Smith

66 Fordham

67 Armory "Slats" Gill

68 Rich Daly, longtime Missouri assistant

69 Jerry Tarkanian, of UNLV (at the time of the quote)

70 Four: 1963-64,1966-67,1971-72 and 1972-73

2-PT **71** What college did Bobby Knight attend?

3-PT **72** Who was the first coach to win an NBA championship after directing a team to the Final Four?

3-PT **73** Who replaced Al McGuire as head basketball coach at Marquette in 1977?

3-PT **74** Who passed away in Lawrence, Kansas, on November 28, 1939?

3-PT **75** Joe B. Hall coached at Kentucky for 13 seasons between 1973 and 1985. At what other two schools did he serve as head coach?

2-PT **76** Hugh Durham, Joe Williams, Steve Robinson and Pat Kennedy have all taken what school to the NCAA tournament?

2-PT **77** Who succeeded Eddie Sutton as the coach at the University of Kentucky?

3-PT **78** Who was the first college division I coach inducted into the Basketball Hall of Fame?

3-PT **79** Where did the great coach Ralph Miller begin his collegiate coaching career?

3-PT **80** At what university have both Rick Pitino and Mike Jarvis been the head basketball coach?

2-PT **81** How many times did Al McGuire lead his teams to the Final Four?

2-PT **82** Who was Marquette's coach when they won the NCAA title in 1977?

3-PT **83** Who said, after losing to Texas A&M in double overtime in the 1980 NCAA tournament: "If Texas A&M wins the national championship, I want people to remember that we tied them twice?"

3-PT **84** Who preceded Norm Stewart as the head coach at Missouri?

71 Ohio State

72 Jack Ramsay led Portland to the NBA crown in 1977 after having led St. Joseph's to the Final Four in 1961.

73 Hank Raymonds

74 Dr. James Naismith

75 Regis and Central Missouri State

76 Florida State

77 Rick Pitino, on June 2, 1989. He left Kentucky to coach the Boston Celtics in 1997.

78 Arad McCutchan, of Evansville

79 Wichita State, in 1951

80 Boston University

81 Twice: Marquette, in 1974 and 1977

82 Al McGuire

83 Dean Smith

84 Bob Vanatta

2-PT **85** Paul Westhead took what team to the NCAA tournament in 1988, 1989 and 1990?

3-PT **86** Who succeeded the legendary Dr. Phog Allen as the coach at the University of Kansas?

2-PT **87** What coach has the most wins at Marquette University?

2-PT **88** Name one of the three teams Joe Williams has taken to the NCAA tournament.

2-PT **89** What university did Rick Pitino attend?

3-PT **90** Former Vanderbilt and Alabama coach C.M. Newton began his coaching career at what school?

2-PT **91** How many Final Fours did Jim Valvano take North Carolina State to?

3-PT **92** What school did Hall of Famer Arthur "Dutch" Lonborg coach from 1928 to 1950, while compiling a record of 236 wins and 203 losses?

2-PT **93** What two coaches met in the 1953 NCAA championship game featuring the University of Kansas and Indiana University?

2-PT **94** Where was Denny Crum an assistant coach before being named head coach at Louisville in 1972?

3-PT **95** What four coaches have taken at least two Kansas teams to the Final Four?

3-PT **96** The legendary Red Auerbach, the president of the Boston Celtics and the winningest coach in NBA history, led what school in scoring during the 1939-40 season?

2-PT **97** Purdue coach Gene Keady graduated from what university?

3-PT **98** Where did Gene Keady coach in 1980?

85 Loyola Marymount

86 Dick Harp, who later resigned to become the President of the Fellowship of Christian Athletes.

87 Al McGuire

88 Jacksonville, Furman and Florida State

89 The University of Massachusetts, class of 1974

90 Transylvania, in 1956

91 One, in 1983, when they won the national championship.

92 Northwestern

93 Phog Allen, of Kansas, and Branch McCracken, of Indiana

94 The University of California-Los Angeles (UCLA)

95 Phog Allen, Larry Brown, Ted Owens and Roy Williams

96 George Washington

97 Kansas State University

98 Western Kentucky

2-PT **99** Who became the coach at Seton Hall University in 1982?

2-PT **100** What coach led North Carolina State to the 1983 NCAA title?

3-PT **101** What coach led Kansas State to the NCAA Final Four in 1958 and 1964?

3-PT **102** Jim Harrick, of UCLA, and Dale Brown, of LSU, both served as assistants at what school?

2-PT **103** Who is the only coach to have lost more than seven Final Four games?

2-PT **104** Name three of the seven coaches to earn a trip to the Final Four in their first season as a head coach.

2-PT **105** Eddie Fogler, Bill Guthridge and Roy Williams have been assistant coaches at what university?

2-PT **106** What three teams has Dave Bliss taken to the NCAA tournament?

2-PT **107** Ben Carnevale, John Wilson and Paul Evans are the winningest coaches at what university?

3-PT **108** Who is the only coach to accumulate losing NCAA tournament records at three different schools?

3-PT **109** Ed Diddle won 759 games as the coach of what university?

2-PT **110** Former Boston Celtics coach Chris Ford played at what university?

3-PT **111** Who coached Detroit-Mercy to its first NCAA tournament win?

2-PT **112** At what two schools has John MacLeod served as head coach?

99 P. J. Carlesimo, who went on to coach the Portland Trailblazers in the NBA.

100 Jim Valvano

101 Tex Winter

102 Utah State

103 Dean Smith

104 Ray Meyer (1943), Gary Thompson (1965), Denny Crum (1972), Bill Hodges (1979), Larry Brown (1980), Steve Fisher (1989) and Bill Guthridge (1998)

105 The University of North Carolina

106 Oklahoma, Southern Methodist and New Mexico

107 Navy

108 George Raveling, who has losing tournament records at Washington State, Iowa and Southern Cal.

109 Western Kentucky

110 Villanova

111 Dick Vitale

112 Oklahoma and Notre Dame

Tex Winter

113 What 1956 graduate of Vermont coached the UNLV Runnin' Rebels?

 114 What coach implemented the four corners offense?

 115 What is Maryland coach Gary Williams's alma mater?

 116 At what university did NBA coach Bill Fitch coach from 1968 through 1970?

 117 Who is the winningest coach in St. John's history: Lou Carnesecca, Al DeStefano or Joe Lapchick?

 118 In 1990, Lon Kruger became the head basketball coach at the University of Florida. At what school did Kruger coach immediately before going to Florida?

 119 Who is the first coach with as many as twenty-five NCAA tournament victories to earn his wins at more than one school?

 120 Where did Jud Heathcote serve as head coach before joining Michigan State in 1977?

 121 Who was the second coach to win back-to-back NCAA championships?

 122 NBA coach Jerry Sloan is a graduate of what university?

 123 What former Western Kentucky coach was the third pick in the 1967 NBA draft?

 124 What three teams has Gene Bartow taken to the NCAA tournament?

 125 Who preceded John Wooden as basketball coach at UCLA?

 126 What team has been led to the NCAA tournament by Doug Mills, Harry Combs and Lou Henson?

127 Who is the only coach to leave an NCAA champion before the next season for another coaching job?

113 Rollie Massimino

114 Dean Smith, of North Carolina

115 The University of Maryland

116 Minnesota

117 Lou Carnesecca

118 His alma mater, Kansas State University. He later left Florida to be the head coach at the University of Illinois.

119 Jerry Tarkanian, of Long Beach State and the University of Nevada-Las Vegas

120 Montana

121 Adolph Rupp, of Kentucky

122 The University of Evansville

123 Clem Haskins, now head coach at Minnesota and 1996-97 NABC coach of the year

124 Memphis State, UCLA and Alabama-Birmingham

125 Wilbur Johns

126 Illinois

127 Larry Brown, who left Kansas before the 1988-1989 season.

128 Marv Harshman was a head coach for 40 seasons with three different schools, the last being Washington. Name one of the other two.

 129 What school has been led to the NCAA tournament by Matt Zunic, Rick Pitino and Mike Jarvis?

 130 Former Virginia Tech, Wyoming, Tennessee and Florida coach Don DeVoe played at what university?

 131 Did Bobby Knight ever win a national championship as a player?

 132 Dean Smith came to North Carolina from what school?

 133 Who is the winningest coach in Alabama history?

 134 Who was Nebraska's coach when the team made its first appearance in the NCAA tournament in 1986?

 135 Who is the only coach to take teams to the Final Four in four different decades?

 136 Where did Tom Heinsohn, a former Celtics coach, play collegiately?

 137 What school did basketball coaching legends and Hall-of-Famers Dr. Forrest Allen, Arthur "Dutch" Lonborg, Adolph Rupp, Dean Smith and Ralph Miller attend?

 138 Who was head basketball coach at the University of Alabama from the 1981-82 season through the 1992-93 season?

 139 Who coached Ohio State to the 1960 national championship?

 140 What two coaches share the record of most years with 42 at one school?

 141 At what school did Dr. Glenn Wilkes coach to become one of the top 25 winningest coaches in Division I basketball?

128 Pacific Lutheran and Washington State

129 Boston University

130 Ohio State University

131 Yes: Ohio State won the national championship in 1960.

132 The United States Air Force Academy located near Colorado Springs, Colorado

133 Wimp Sanderson, with 267 victories

134 Moe Iba, son of legendary coach Hank Iba

135 Dean Smith

136 Holy Cross

137 The University of Kansas

138 Wimp Sanderson

139 Fred Taylor

140 Ed Diddle, of Western Kentucky, and Ray Meyer, of DePaul

141 Stetson University

Ed Diddle

CHAPTER 3
I DIDN'T KNOW THAT...

 1 Who was the only native of Indiana among the starting five on the Hoosiers' 1987 national championship team?

 2 What is the only former NCAA champion that is no longer classified as a Division I college?

 3 What university did Dick Vitale attend?

 4 This basketball staple was first used in 1914. What is this staple known as?

 5 What is the nation's oldest athletic conference?

 6 In what year was basketball invented?

 7 Former Miami (Florida) great Rick Barry has four sons who have played college basketball. Name the three schools they played for.

 8 Who played in the first Basketball Hall of Fame Tip-Off Classic on November 17, 1979, in Springfield, Massachusetts?

 9 Who won the first college basketball game ever played in the state of North Carolina?

 10 What was part of the official flight kit of the space shuttle Discovery on March 13, 1989?

 11 What was the first school in NCAA history to jump from a junior college mens basketball program to a four-year NCAA Division I program?

 12 David Adkins averaged 4.2 points and 4.4 rebounds during his varsity career at Denver. What's the big deal?

1   Steve Alford

2   City College of New York

3   Mr. Vitale graduated from Seton Hall in 1962.

4   The net

5   The Southern Conference, founded in 1921.

6   Dr. James Naismith invented the game of basketball in the winter of 1891 in Springfield, Massachusetts.

7   Scooter played for Kansas, Jon and Drew for Georgia Tech, and Brent for Oregon State.

8   Duke defeated Kentucky 82-76.

9   Wake Forest defeated Trinity, which is now Duke, 15-5 on March 2, 1906.

10   An official Spalding Hall of Fame basketball

11   Weber State, in 1962-63

12   David Adkins is also known as Sinbad, the actor and television personality.

13 Who presented the Olympic medals to the medal-winning teams at the 1936 Olympics played in Berlin?

 14 What two schools have had two different players lead the nation in scoring in consecutive years?

 15 What is the only school to be denied three NCAA tournament berths because it was on probation?

 16 What conference saw all five of its entrants lose their first round games in the NCAA tournament in 1989?

 17 What was the first college season in which seven players had scoring averages of 30 points or better per game? Was it 1964, 1967, 1970, or 1973?

 18 What is the southernmost team in the Big East Conference?

 19 Who was the first team to win more than one NCAA championship and also the NIT?

 20 What former Virginia Cavalier basketball player also played in the NFL as a quarterback for the Kansas City Chiefs?

 21 What kind of ball was used during the first three years of basketball?

 22 The great Jackie Robinson is the only four-sport, including basketball, letter winner at what school?

 23 Who is the only basketball coach with a losing record at the University of Kansas?

 24 Starting in 1938, name four NCAA Division I schools that have finished a season undefeated. (Hint - not all of them competed in the NCAA tournament.)

 25 On July 1, 1988, the Pacific Coast Athletic Association became what conference?

13 Dr. James Naismith, the man who invented the game, presented the medals and witnessed the world-wide growth of basketball.

14 Furman and Loyola Marymount. For Furman, Frank Selvy ('54) and Darrall Floyd ('55). For Loyola Marymount, Hank Gathers ('89) and Bo Kimble ('90).

15 North Carolina State in 1955, 1959 and 1973

16 The Southeastern Conference

17 1964

18 The University of Miami (Florida)

19 Kentucky

20 Matt Blundin

21 Dr. James Naismith selected a soccer ball and peach baskets were used for the goals.

22 The University of California-Los Angeles

23 James Naismith, the inventor of the game, compiled a record of 55 wins and 60 losses while at Kansas. Naismith, however, didn't travel to many games and really didn't endorse the concept of coaching the game.

24 L.I.U. – Brooklyn, Army, Seton Hall, Kentucky, San Francisco, North Carolina, UCLA, North Carolina State and Indiana

25 The Big West

2-PT **26** In how many NCAA tournaments did Pete Maravich compete?

3-PT **27** What was the first conference to experiment with the three-point basket?

3-PT **28** What university qualified for the NCAA tournament in 1993 thereby making its state the last to have an eligible basketball team qualify?

3-PT **29** What position did Dean Smith play in baseball at Kansas?

3-PT **30** What 1992 Oklahoma State player was drafted by both the Chicago Bulls and the Kansas City Chiefs?

3-PT **31** Cawood Ledford is known for being the great radio announcer and personality for what university?

3-PT **32** What two teams participated in the first televised NCAA championship game?

2-PT **33** What is the first state to have more than six different schools reach the Final Four?

3-PT **34** Who is the only player among the top twenty all-time tournament scorers to go scoreless in a NCAA tournament game?

2-PT **35** What school beat eventual 1989 national champion Michigan twice during the regular season, both times by more than 12 points?

3-PT **36** The first basketball backboards were made of what material?

2-PT **37** The 1937-38 season saw Rhode Island State become the highest scoring team in the country. Did Rhode Island State average 50, 60, or 70 points a game?

3-PT **38** What player has performed for two different teams in the NCAA championship game?

26 None, his teams failed to qualify for the NCAA tournament.

27 The Southern Conference, in 1980

28 University of Delaware

29 Catcher

30 Corey Williams

31 The University of Kentucky

32 La Salle defeated Bradley 92 - 76 in the finals in 1954.

33 Pennsylvania with Duquesne, La Salle, Pennsylvania, Penn State, St. Joseph's, Temple and Villanova

34 Danny Ferry, of Duke, did not score against Texas A&M in a 1987 tournament game.

35 Illinois

36 The first backboards were made of wire mesh.

37 70

38 Bob Bender played in the 1976 championship game for Indiana and in the 1978 game for Duke.

39 Since the inception of the Associated Press poll in 1949, UCLA has captured eight season-end number-one rankings, the same number as what other university?

40 Major league baseball great Dick Groat was also one of the leading scorers in the country in college basketball. At what school did Dick Groat play?

41 In 1949, the Associated Press introduced its nationwide college poll. Who was the first team voted number one in the poll?

42 Ted Cassidy, who played Lurch on the Addams Family, played basketball at what university?

43 What was the first school to win more than 1,200 games and not reach the Final Four?

44 Who were the first father and son to play for teams from the same school that reached the NCAA title game?

 45 What does ACC stand for?

 46 How many players were on the first basketball teams in the games played at Springfield?

 47 What is the only Michigan school to lead the nation in scoring in Division I?

39 The University of Kentucky

40 Duke University

41 The University of Kentucky

42 Stetson University

43 Fordham

44 Gene Elstun played for Kansas in 1957 as his son, Doug, did in 1991.

45 Atlantic Coast Conference

46 Nine. Naismith had 18 students in his YMCA physical education class and he split the group in half.

47 The Detroit Mercy Titans averaged 96.1 points per game in 1964.

CHAPTER 4
NICKNAMES

1-PT 1 What is the nickname of Illinois State University?

1-PT 2 What is the nickname of the University of South Carolina ?

2-PT 3 What school's basketball team is nicknamed the Greyhounds?

3-PT 4 What school's basketball team is nicknamed the Delta Devils?

3-PT 5 Who was nicknamed "The Rocket?"

3-PT 6 What is Grambling's team nickname?

3-PT 7 What school's basketball team is nicknamed the Salukis?

3-PT 8 What school's basketball team is nicknamed the Redskins?

2-PT 9 What school's basketball team is nicknamed the Red Flash?

2-PT 10 What school's basketball team is nicknamed the Phoenix?

3-PT 11 Who was "Doctor Dunkenstein?"

3-PT 12 What player nicknamed Wah Wah played forward as one of Kentucky's Fabulous Five in 1948 and 1949?

3-PT 13 What school's basketball team is nicknamed the Moccasins?

1 The Redbirds. At one time Illinois State was known as the Cardinals, but that was changed to Redbirds to avoid confusion with the St. Louis Cardinals baseball team.

2 The Gamecocks. An account of an early football game stated that the South Carolina team "fought like game cocks." A local newspaper shortened the name to one word in 1903 and South Carolina teams have been Gamecocks ever since.

3 Loyola College

4 Mississippi Valley State University

5 Rick Mount, of Purdue

6 The Tigers

7 Southern Illinois University

8 Miami University (Ohio)

9 St. Francis College

10 The University of Wisconsin-Green Bay

11 Darrell Griffith, of the University of Louisville

12 Wallace Jones, who joined with Alex Groza, Ralph Beard, Kenny Rollins and Cliff Barker to form Kentucky's starting lineup.

13 The University of Tennessee-Chattanooga

14 What 6-foot 9-inch Providence center, nicknamed "Bad News," led the nation in rebounding with an 18.7 rebound average in 1974?

 15 What school's basketball team is nicknamed the Spiders?

 16 What is Bowling Green's team nickname?

 17 Two Division I schools are nicknamed the Crusaders. Name one of them.

 18 What school's basketball team is nicknamed the Highlanders?

 19 What school's basketball team is nicknamed the Kangaroos?

 20 What school's basketball team is nicknamed the Peacocks?

 21 What was the nickname of Oklahoma A&M's seven-footer Bob Kurland?

 22 What school's basketball team is nicknamed the Pilots?

 23 What school's basketball team is nicknamed the Quakers?

 24 Four Division I schools are nicknamed the Hawks. Name one of them.

 25 What pair of North Carolina State guards were known as "Fire and Ice?"

 26 What is the nickname of Purdue University?

 27 What school's basketball team is nicknamed the Aztecs?

28 What is East Tennessee State's team nickname?

14 Marvin Barnes

15 The University of Richmond

16 The Falcons. A local sportswriter penned the name because it fit headline space well and falcons are a powerful bird for their size.

17 Holy Cross and Valparaiso

18 Radford University

19 The University of Missouri-Kansas City

20 St. Peter's College

21 Foothills

22 The University of Portland

23 The University of Pennsylvania

24 University of Hartford, Maryland Eastern Shore, Monmouth College and St. Joseph's

25 Rodney Monroe and Chris Corchiani

26 The Boilermakers. At one time, teams representing Purdue were called cornfield sailors, blacksmiths, pumpkin shuckers, hayseeds, farmers and rail splitters.

27 San Diego State University

28 The Buccaneers

29 What player nicknamed Mookie led Oklahoma to the NCAA title game in 1988?

 30 Two Division I schools are nicknamed the Seahawks. Name one of them.

 31 What school's basketball team is nicknamed the Jaspers?

 32 What school's basketball team is nicknamed the Saints?

 33 What school's basketball team is nicknamed the Fighting Camels?

 34 What school's basketball team is nicknamed the Billikens?

 35 What school's basketball team is nicknamed the Toreros?

 36 What is the nickname of the University of California–Los Angeles?

 37 What school's basketball team is nicknamed the Dons?

 38 What was the nickname of Stanford University when it won the national title in 1942?

 39 What is the nickname of Oregon State University?

 40 What is the nickname of the University of Louisville?

 41 What school's basketball team is nicknamed the Cardinal?

29 Daron Blaylock was the point guard for coach Billy Tubbs in the championship game against Kansas in Kansas City, Missouri.

30 North Carolina-Wilmington and Wagner College

31 Manhattan College

32 Siena College

33 Campbell University

34 St. Louis University

35 The University of San Diego

36 The Bruins. Back in 1919 when UCLA was known as the Southern Branch of the University of California, the football team was known as the Cubs because of its younger relationship to Berkeley Bears. Later, that was changed to the Grizzlies. When the school joined the Pacific Coast Conference in 1928, Montana was already called the Grizzlies, so the name was changed to the Bruins.

37 The University of San Francisco

38 The Indians

39 The Beavers. The name comes from the official moniker of the state of Oregon, which is known as the Beaver State.

40 The Cardinals. The Cardinal is the state bird of Kentucky.

41 Stanford University

42 What school's basketball team is nicknamed the Buffaloes?

 43 What school's basketball team is nicknamed the Golden Griffins?

 44 What school's basketball team is nicknamed the Vikings?

 45 What were the real names of Jacksonville's 1970 center and guard who were known as Batman and Robin?

 46 Name two schools that are nicknamed the Eagles.

 47 What school's basketball team is nicknamed the Dragons?

 48 What school's basketball team is nicknamed the Black Bears?

 49 What school's basketball team is nicknamed the Chanticleers?

 50 What is Austin Peay's team nickname?

 51 What school's basketball team is nicknamed the Leathernecks?

 52 What school's basketball team is nicknamed the Retrievers?

 53 What school's basketball team is nicknamed the Demons?

 54 What school's basketball team is nicknamed the Red Foxes?

 55 What type of animal has the honor of being a mascot for the Army Cadets?

56 What is Furman's team nickname?

42 The University of Colorado

43 Canisius College

44 Cleveland State University

45 Artis Gilmore and Rex Morgan

46 American University, Boston College, Coppin State, Eastern Michigan, Eastern Washington, Georgia Southern, Morehead State and Winthrop College

47 Drexel University

48 The University of Maine

49 Coastal Carolina College

50 The Governors. Named for a former Tennessee governor.

51 Western Illinois University

52 Maryland Baltimore County

53 Northwestern State University

54 Marist College

55 While Army is commonly called the Black Knights, a mule has been the official mascot since 1899. The choice of the mule reflects the long-standing usefulness of the animal in military operations.

56 The Paladins. Furman athletic teams were known by different names until the 1961 school year. The baseball team was the Hornets, the football team the Hurricanes and the basketball team the Paladins.

3-PT **57** What school's basketball team is nicknamed the Stags?

3-PT **58** What is Dayton's team nickname?

3-PT **59** What school's basketball team is nicknamed the Ramblers?

2-PT **60** What school's basketball team is nicknamed the Golden Panthers?

3-PT **61** What is Cal-State Fullerton's team nickname?

1-PT **62** See if you can top this. What is the nickname of Stetson University?

3-PT **63** What school's basketball team is nicknamed the Rattlers?

3-PT **64** What is Marshall's team nickname?

1-PT **65** What school's basketball team is nicknamed the Green Wave?

1-PT **66** What is the nickname of Northwestern University?

2-PT **67** What school's basketball team is nicknamed the Blackbirds?

1-PT **68** What school's basketball team is nicknamed the Big Green?

3-PT **69** What school's basketball team is nicknamed the Leopards?

2-PT **70** What school was originally known as Latter Day Saints University?

3-PT **71** "The Tall Firs" was the adopted nickname of what early national champion?

57 Fairfield University

58 The Flyers. Dayton is known as the birthplace of aviation and the home of the Wright Brothers.

59 Loyola University

60 Florida International University

61 The Titans

62 The Hatters

63 Florida A&M University

64 The Thundering Herd. A former sports editor and columnist of the *Huntington Herald-Dispatch* took the name from the title of one of Zane Grey's western novels.

65 Tulane University

66 The Wildcats

67 Long Island University

68 Dartmouth College

69 Lafayette College

70 Brigham Young University

71 The 1939 national championship Oregon team

72 What nickname is used by more Division I basketball programs than any other?

 73 What school's basketball team is nicknamed the Gauchos?

 74 What player nicknamed "Cornbread" helped North Carolina-Charlotte to the NCAA tournament in 1977?

 75 What player nicknamed Big Daddy played center for Texas Western's NCAA title team in 1966?

 76 What school's basketball team is nicknamed the Dolphins?

 77 What school's basketball team is nicknamed the Blue Raiders?

 78 What school's basketball team is nicknamed the Golden Flashes?

 79 What school's basketball team is nicknamed the Chippewas?

 80 What school's basketball team is nicknamed the Matadors?

 81 What school's basketball team is nicknamed the Bonnies?

 82 What school's basketball team is nicknamed the Waves?

 83 What player nicknamed "The Glyde" led Houston to the NCAA Final Four in 1982 and 1983?

 84 Two Division I schools are nicknamed the Bulls. Name one of them.

 85 What school's basketball team is nicknamed the Mean Green?

 86 What school's basketball team is nicknamed the Razorbacks?

72 Bulldogs, which is the nickname of twelve schools

73 The University of California-Santa Barbara

74 Cedric Maxwell

75 David Lattin, who played a significant role in helping the Miners defeat Kentucky for the national championship.

76 Jacksonville University

77 Middle Tennesse State University

78 Kent State University

79 Central Michigan University

80 Cal State-Northridge

81 St. Bonaventure University

82 Pepperdine University

83 Clyde Drexler

84 University of Buffalo and South Florida

85 The University of North Texas

86 The University of Arkansas

87 Nine Division I schools are nicknamed the Wildcats. Name four of them.

 88 What player nicknamed Butch led Marquette to the NCAA Final Four in 1977?

 89 What is the nickname of Florida State University?

 90 What is the nickname of the University of Maryland?

 91 What school's basketball team is nicknamed the Hokies?

 92 What school's basketball team is nicknamed the Mavericks?

 93 What was the nickname of Jack Givens, the MOP on Kentucky's 1978 NCAA title team?

 94 What is the nickname of Princeton University?

 95 What school's basketball team is nicknamed the Orangemen?

 96 Who were the five starters on the Phi Slamma Jamma Houston team of 1983?

 97 Who is also known as "The General?"

 98 What school's basketball team is nicknamed the Blue Hens?

 99 What school's basketball team is nicknamed the Horned Frogs?

 100 What school's basketball team is nicknamed the Rockets?

87 Arizona, Bethune-Cookman College, Davidson, Kansas State, Kentucky, New Hampshire, Northwestern, Villanova and Weber State

88 Alfred Lee

89 The Seminoles. The influence of the first Americans has left its impact on the nickname for teams at Florida State.

90 The Terrapins. The Terrapin first appeared at Maryland in 1922, when the campus newspaper was looking for a new name. The school's president recommended Diamondback in honor of the state's famed Diamondback Terrapin. Soon afterwards, the teams became known as the Terrapins.

91 Virginia Tech

92 The University of Texas-Arlington

93 Goose

94 The Tigers

95 Syracuse University

96 Drexler, Micheaux, Olajuwon, Franklin and Young

97 University of Indiana Coach Bobby Knight

98 University of Delaware

99 Texas Christian University

100 The University of Toledo

CHAPTER 5
PLACES

3-PT **1** UAB Arena is the home court for what college basketball team?

2-PT **2** In what city was the 1990 Final Four held?

2-PT **3** What arena was chosen to host the 1996 Final Four?

2-PT **4** In what city was the 1985 Final Four held?

3-PT **5** The Oquirrh Bucket is presented to the best college basketball team in what state each year?

3-PT **6** What is the home arena of Wake Forest University?

3-PT **7** What arena is the home court of Butler University?

2-PT **8** What is the home court of the University of Louisville Cardinals?

2-PT **9** In what city did Kentucky beat Duke to win the 1978 NCAA title?

3-PT **10** What building served as the home of the Kentucky Wildcats before Rupp Arena?

3-PT **11** In what arena does Evansville play its home games?

2-PT **12** Name the only team from the state of Texas to have won the national championship.

3-PT **13** In what state is Appalachian State?

2-PT **14** Where is the University of Alabama located?

1 University of Alabama-Birmingham

2 Denver, Colorado

3 The Meadowlands Arena

4 Lexington, Kentucky

5 Utah

6 Lawrence Joel Veterans Memorial Coliseum in Winston-Salem, North Carolina

7 Hinkle Fieldhouse

8 Freedom Hall

9 St. Louis, Missouri

10 Memorial Coliseum

11 Roberts Stadium

12 The University of Texas-El Paso, in 1966 known as Texas Western in championship year of 1966.

13 North Carolina (Boone)

14 Tuscaloosa

3-PT **15** In what arena does North Carolina State play its home games? Clue: wrap it up.

3-PT **16** What two teams played the first college game ever in Madison Square Garden?

3-PT **17** Barnhill Arena had been the home of the Arkansas Razorbacks since 1957. What successful businessman is their new arena named after?

2-PT **18** Four schools from the District of Columbia play men's basketball in NCAA Division I. Name two of them.

3-PT **19** In what state is Yale located?

3-PT **20** Name one of the two men Oklahoma State's basketball arena is named after.

2-PT **21** In what city was the 1988 Final Four held?

2-PT **22** In what city did Marquette beat North Carolina when they won the 1977 NCAA title?

2-PT **23** What was the first domed stadium to hold a Final Four?

3-PT **24** In what arena did North Carolina State upset Houston to win the 1983 national championship?

3-PT **25** What arena is the home court for the University of Alabama?

2-PT **26** In what city was the 1984 Final Four held?

3-PT **27** In what arena does Houston play its home games?

3-PT **28** Temple University called this hall home.

1-PT **29** Where is the Basketball Hall of Fame located?

15 Reynolds Coliseum

16 St. John's and City College of New York, in 1931

17 Bud Walton, a principal in the Wal-Mart empire

18 American, Georgetown, George Washington and Howard

19 Connecticut (New Haven)

20 Gallagher-Iba Arena is named after wrestling coach Edward C. Gallagher and basketball coaching legend Henry P. Iba.

21 In Kansas City, Missouri. This was the 50th anniversary of the championship and ironically the score was tied 50-50 at halftime.

22 In 1977, the men's basketball team won its first NCAA men's basketball title in Atlanta, Georgia.

23 The Houston Astrodome

24 At University Arena, also known as "The Pit," home of New Mexico University.

25 Coleman Coliseum

26 Seattle, Washington

27 Hofheinz Pavilion

28 McGonigle

29 Springfield, Massachusetts

30 What city was chosen to host the 1994 Final Four?

 31 In what arena does Iowa play its home games?

 32 In what state would you find Campbell University?

 33 What city were the five starters on the 1957 national champion North Carolina team from?

 34 On December 21, 1980, which country hosted the first official NCAA game ever played outside the U.S., in which UCLA defeated Temple?

 35 Columbia University is located in what city?

 36 In what state would you find Hofstra University?

 37 Why was there a black tie affair on the campus of Springfield College on December 21, 1991?

 38 In what city was Lew Alcindor born?

 39 In what state would you find Gonzaga University?

 40 In what town is the University of Oklahoma located?

 41 In what state is Murray State?

 42 In what arena does Clemson play its home games?

 43 What is Harvard's homecourt?

 44 In what state would you find the College of William and Mary?

30 Charlotte, North Carolina

31 Carver Hawkeye

32 North Carolina

33 New York, New York

34 Japan hosted the game in the city of Tokyo.

35 New York, New York

36 New York (Hempstead)

37 To celebrate the hundredth birthday of the invention of the game.

38 New York, New York

39 Gonzaga University, founded in 1887, is located in Spokane Washington.

40 Norman

41 Kentucky

42 Littlejohn Coliseum

43 The Lavietes Basketball Pavilion at the Briggs Athletic Center, the nation's third-oldest Division I facility for basketball, is now named for Ray Lavietes, a 1936 graduate and two-year letterman for the Crimson.

44 Virginia

45 Name the eight states represented in the Big 10 conference.

 46 In what fieldhouse does the University of Maryland play its home games?

 47 Lehigh is located in what state?

 48 In what arena does the University of Michigan play its home games?

 49 Northwestern University is located in what city?

 50 What does NCAA stand for?

 51 In what city did Indiana win the NCAA title in 1976?

 52 What fieldhouse does the University of Kansas call home?

 53 What city was chosen to host the 1995 Final Four?

 54 Columbia, Missouri is home to what university?

 55 In what city was the 1986 Final Four held?

 56 In what city is Duke University located?

 57 What is the only state with at least seven Division I schools to never have a team reach the Final Four?

 58 Where is Holt Arena, the first arena constructed on a college campus which could house both football and basketball games?

86 Illinois, Indiana, Iowa, Michigan, Minnesota, Ohio, Pennsylvania and Wisconsin

46 Cole Fieldhouse

47 Pennsylvania

48 Crisler Arena

49 Evanston, Illinois

50 National Collegiate Athletic Association

51 Philadelphia, Pennsylvania

52 In Allen Fieldhouse where a crowd of 17,228 Jayhawks fans cheered as KU defeated the Kansas State Wildcats 77-66 in the first game at the arena in 1955. Five million fans later, the fieldhouse remains one of the best atmospheres for college basketball.

53 Seattle, Washington

54 The University of Missouri

55 Dallas, Texas

56 In Durham, North Carolina

57 South Carolina

58 Idaho State

Allen Fieldhouse

3-PT   **59** The Thundering Herd of Marshall are located in what state?

2-PT   **60** What city hosted the NCAA six straight years from 1943 to 1949?

3-PT   **62** In what arena does Iowa State play its home games?

2-PT   **63** In what city is Texas Christian University located?

3-PT   **64** Where is Cornell?

2-PT   **65** In what town is the University of Nebraska located?

2-PT   **66** In what city and state is Drexel University?

1-PT   **67** Where is the University of Tennessee located?

3-PT   **68** Where does Arizona State play its home games?

3-PT   **69** In what city is Duquesne located?

3-PT   **70** In what state is McNeese State?

2-PT   **71** The University of Washington is located in what city?

3-PT   **72** What was the name of the town in Indiana that Larry Bird grew up in?

3-PT   **73** What Big 10 school had the first basketball gymnasium known as a fieldhouse?

2-PT   **74** Where is Auburn University?

59 West Virginia

60 New York, New York

62 Hilton Coliseum

63 Fort Worth, Texas

64 Ithaca, New York

65 Lincoln

66 Philadelphia, Pennsylvania

67 Knoxville, Tennessee

68 University Activity Center

69 The same place that Heinz ketchup and Mister Rogers' Neighborhood come from: Pittsburgh, Pennsylvania.

70 Louisiana

71 Seattle

72 French Lick, Indiana

73 Michigan, with Yost Fieldhouse

74 Auburn University is located in east-central Alabama in Lee County. The city of Auburn, founded in 1836 by Judge John Harper, has a population of about 35,000. The name was derived from the line "Sweet Auburn, loveliest village of the Plain" in Oliver Goldsmith's poem "The Deserted Village."

3-PT **75** The 1980-81 season brought a new home court to the University of Florida. Name that home court.

3-PT **76** Where is Howard University?

2-PT **77** In what city is the University of Illinois located?

3-PT **78** Where is Fordham?

3-PT **79** In what state would you find Holy Cross?

3-PT **80** What is the home court of Harvard?

2-PT **81** Who was chosen to host the 1997 Final Four?

3-PT **82** In what arena does Oregon State University play its home games?

2-PT **83** Florida International is located in what city in Florida?

2-PT **84** In what city is Vanderbilt University located?

2-PT **85** Bradley is located in what state?

75 The Stephen C. O'Connell Center

76 Washington, D.C.

77 The University of Illinois, chartered in 1867 as a land-grant institution, is located in Urbana-Champaign.

78 Fordham University has residential campuses at Rose Hill in the north Bronx and Lincoln Center in Manhattan, as well as academic centers in Tarrytown and Armonk, New York.

79 Massachusetts

80 Briggs Athletic Center

81 Indianapolis, Indiana

82 Gill Coliseum

83 Miami

84 Vanderbilt University is located in Nashville, a major city in the southern portion of the United States and the capital of Tennessee.

85 Illinois (Peoria)

CHAPTER 6
PLAYERS

 1 Who was the first player to score over 40 points in the NCAA championship game?

 2 Who was the NCAA tournament MOP in 1979 and the NBA Finals MVP in 1980, 1982 and 1987?

 3 What former Los Angeles Laker guard is the second all-time leading scorer at Duquesne?

 4 What Morehead State standout led the nation in scoring in 1992 with a 28.1 point average?

 5 Who was the first player in NCAA history to have a career scoring average in excess of 40 points per game?

 6 Wayman Tisdale played collegiately at what university?

 7 What 6-foot 7-inch Creighton player lead the nation in rebounding in 1963 and finished his career averaging more than 21 rebounds per game?

 8 What was Hank Gathers' given first name?

 9 What Texas Longhorn player was the first to surpass 2,000 career points, playing from 1987 through 1990?

 10 Pervis Ellison attended what university?

 11 Who was named the NCAA tournament's Most Outstanding Player in 1958?

 12 Earl Wise, Stephen Kite, Frank Jones and Anthony Avery are four of the leading scorers at what university?

 13 Where did Danny Ainge play collegiately?

1 Gail Goodrich, of the University of California-Los Angeles, scored 42 points in 1965 to help his team defeat Michigan 91-80.

2 Magic Johnson of Michigan State University and the Los Angeles Lakers

3 Norm Nixon

4 Brett Roberts

5 Pete Maravich, of LSU, averaged 44.2 points per game.

6 Oklahoma

7 Paul Silas had 1,751 rebounds during three seasons. (1962-64)

8 Eric

9 Travis Mays

10 The University of Louisville

11 Elgin Baylor, of Seattle

12 Tennessee Tech

13 Brigham Young

Gail Goodrich

14 In what categories did Xavier McDaniel of Wichita State lead the nation in 1985?

 15 For what team did Rony Seikaly play in the 1987 Final Four?

 16 Name one of the two national scoring champions that Texas-Pan American has produced.

 17 In 1990, Danny Jones became the all-time leading scorer at what Big 10 university?

 18 Jim Lacey, of Loyola-Maryland, was the first player in NCAA Division I history to do what?

 19 Tom Morgan, Fly Williams and Otis Howard are the leading career scorers at what school?

 20 This Arizona Wildcat has played in a Final Four and led the American league in stolen bases.

 21 What position did Larry Bird play at Indiana State?

 22 What great Kansas center left school early to play for the Harlem Globetrotters?

 23 Where did Mark Price play collegiately?

 24 Who was the first player to average over 40 points per game for a season?

 25 ABA and NBA veteran Ron Boone attended what university?

14 "X-man" averaged 27.2 points and 14.8 rebounds per game to lead the nation in both categories.

15 Syracuse

16 Marshall Rogers and Greg Guy

17 The University of Wisconsin

18 Score over 2,000 points in his career

19 Austin Peay State University

20 Kenny Lofton averaged 4.8 points and 2.6 assists in his 4 years at Arizona.

21 Forward

22 Wilt Chamberlain

32 Georgia Tech

24 Frank Selvy, of Furman, averaged 41.7 points per game in 1954.

25 Idaho State. His son Jaron attended Nebraska.

Wilt Chamberlain

26 Where did Tom Gola play collegiately?

 27 Dan Majerle played where collegiately?

 28 What Duke star made a last-second shot to beat Connecticut in the 1990 East Regionals?

 29 Who passed Don Fleming to become Harvard's leading scorer in basketball history?

 30 What 6-foot 3-inch Seton Hall player led the nation in scoring as a junior in 1963 with a 29.5 average, the lowest average of his varsity career?

 31 Who became the all-time leading scorer in Ohio State basketball history in 1987, with 2,096 points?

 32 Who is the only player in Maryland history to lead the team in scoring three straight years?

 33 What position did Wilt Chamberlain play at Kansas?

 34 Where did Shaquille O'Neal play collegiately?

 35 Who was the first non-guard to be the undisputed leading scorer of the NCAA tournament and not participate in the Final Four?

 36 Mel Henderson, Lafe Mills and Ledell Eackles are the top three leading scorers at what university?

 37 What player from La Salle won the 1990 Adolph Rupp Trophy as the *Associated Press* Player of the Year?

 38 Who was the first college basketball player or coach to be named *The Sporting News* Man of the Year?

 39 Who replaced Lew Alcindor as the starting center at UCLA?

 40 At what university did Clyde Drexler play basketball?

26 LaSalle

27 Central Michigan

28 Christian Laettner

29 Joe Carrabino

30 Nick Werkman

31 Dennis Hopson

32 John Lucas

33 Center

34 Louisiana State

35 Roosevelt Chapman, of Dayton, scored 105 points in four games in 1984.

36 The University of New Orleans

37 Lionel Simmons

38 John Wooden, of UCLA, in 1970

39 Steve Patterson

40 The University of Houston

Steve Patterson

2-PT **41** Who was both the 1987 college Player of the Year and the 1990 NBA Rookie of the Year?

3-PT **42** What 6-foot 4-inch Portland State guard led the nation in scoring in 1977 and 1978?

3-PT **43** At what school did Louie Dampier play from 1965 through 1967?

3-PT **44** Billy McKinney and Jim Stack are the top two career scorers at what school?

3-PT **45** NBA-great Chet Walker attended what university?

3-PT **46** What 6-foot 3-inch Mississippi Valley player led the nation in three-point field goals made per game in 1988 and 1989?

3-PT **47** What 6-foot 3-inch guard was named Most Outstanding Player of the 1959 NCAA tournament?

2-PT **48** Harvey Grant, an All-Conference player at Oklahoma, began his college career at what school?

3-PT **49** Who was the tallest player on Texas Western's 1966 national championship team?

3-PT **50** What two Cincinnati players are in the Basketball Hall of Fame?

3-PT **51** Who was the first player to score 2,000 points in a three-year career?

3-PT **52** What Wake Forest standout finished his career, which lasted from 1984 through 1987, as the school's all-time leader in assists?

2-PT **53** Who became the all-time leading scorer at Georgetown in 1982?

2-PT **54** What LSU player scored 50 points or more 28 times during his career, which lasted from 1968 through 1970?

41 David Robinson

42 Freeman Williams averaged 38.8 in 1977 and 35.9 in 1978.

43 Kentucky

44 Northwestern

45 Bradley

46 Timothy Pollard

47 Jerry West, of West Virginia

48 Clemson

49 Dave "Big Daddy" Lattin, at 6-foot 7-inches

50 Oscar Robertson and Jack Twyman

51 Frank Selvy of Furman, with 2,538 points

52 Tyrone (Muggsy) Bogues

53 Eric "Sleepy" Floyd

54 Pete Maravich

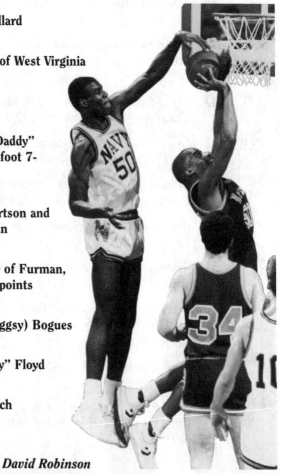

David Robinson

55 Who is the tallest player in Virginia basketball history?

 56 Who holds eight of the top ten highest single-game scoring performances in Houston history?

 57 What Duke player was named the MOP of the 1991 NCAA Final Four?

 58 Bailey Howell played collegiately at what university?

 59 Where was Danny Ferry a collegiate star?

 60 Name two of the three UCLA players drafted in the first round of the 1979 NBA draft.

 61 What three Arkansas players were drafted in the first round of the 1992 NBA draft?

 62 Who was the NCAA tournament's Most Outstanding Player in 1986?

 63 What guard became the all-time leading scorer at Purdue University in 1970?

 64 Who was the shortest player on North Carolina State's 1974 title team?

 65 Who became the first player to score over 2,000 career points at Louisville?

 66 Who was the last player in NCAA history to average at least 20 rebounds per game in a single season?

 67 What position did JoJo White play at the University of Kansas?

 68 Who was the starting center on North Carolina's 1993 national championship team?

69 Where did Bill Laimbeer play collegiately?

55 Ralph Sampson, at 7-foot 4 inches

56 Elvin Hayes

57 Christian Laettner

58 Mississippi State

59 Duke

60 David Greenwood, Roy Hamilton and Brad Holland

61 Todd Day, Lee Mayberry and Oliver Miller

62 Pervis Ellison, of Louisville

63 Rick Mount, with 2,323 points

64 Monte Towe, at 5-foot 7-inches

65 Darrell Griffith

66 Kermit Washington, of American, averaged 20.0 rebounds in 1973.

67 Guard

68 Eric Montross

69 Notre Dame

Jo Jo White

70 What 6-foot 6-inch Mississippi standout led the nation in scoring in 1971 with a 40.1 point average during his only year in Division I basketball?

 71 Where did Kevin McHale play collegiately?

 72 What position did Dave Cowens play for Florida State in 1967-1970?

 73 Who was the first player to score more than 400 career points in the NCAA tournament?

 74 Who was the first Division I college player to score 100 points in a single game?

 75 Who was the first freshman to lead a national champion in scoring?

 76 Merlin Wilson has the highest career rebound average at what university?

 77 Who was the MOP in the 1957 NCAA tournament and the MVP of the NBA Finals in 1972?

 78 Who was the 1987 college basketball Player of the Year?

 79 What 6-foot 10-inch forward played for Memphis State from 1982 to 1985?

 80 Who was the first undergraduate non-center to average more than 23 points per game for a national champion?

 81 Where did Brad Daugherty play collegiately?

 82 Who is the shortest player to ever lead an NCAA champion in scoring?

 83 What LSU Tiger averaged 44.2 points per game in his career?

70 Johnny Neumann

71 Minnesota

72 Center

73 Christian Laettner, of Duke, scored 407 points in the NCAA tournament in his career.

74 Frank Selvy, of Furman, accomplished the feat against Newberry on Feb. 13, 1954.

75 Arnie Ferrin, of Utah, in 1944

76 Georgetown

77 Wilt Chamberlain

78 David Robinson, of Navy

79 Keith Lee

80 David Thompson, of North Carolina State, in 1974

81 North Carolina

82 Five-foot ten-inch Bobby Joe Hill, of Texas Western (now Texas-El Paso), in 1966

83 Pete Maravich

84 What University of Texas player led the nation in rebounding with a 13.5 rebounds per game average in 1981-82?

85 This Wimbledon champion was a reserve on the Cincinnati team in 1951.

86 Name one of the three University of Pittsburgh basketball players who have had their jersey numbers retired from Pitt.

87 Who was the 1992 Player of the Year in the Pac-10?

88 Ronnie Williams, with 2,090 points, is the all-time leading scorer at what school?

89 Hal Greer, an NBA great, played at what university?

90 Who was a two-year consensus All-American for Wake Forest in 1996 and 1997?

91 Which two players that started on Indiana's 1987 national championship team were junior college transfers?

92 Who were the first five players on the NCAA Final Four All-Time Team? Here is a clue: Three played for the Lakers, one for the Celtics and one for the Bulls.

93 At what year in his academic career was Magic Johnson when he led Michigan State to the NCAA title in 1979?

94 Who was born on April 16, 1947, the same day the NBA held its first championship game?

95 What school did 1973 national scoring leader William "Bird" Averitt compete for?

84 LaSalle Thompson, who left school after his junior year and began his pro career with the Kansas City Kings in the NBA.

85 Tony Trabert averaged 6.9 points during the 1951 season.

86 Don Hennon, Charles Smith and Billy Knight

87 Harold Miner, of Southern Cal

88 The University of Florida

89 Marshall

90 Tim Duncan

91 Keith Smart and Dean Garrett

92 Lew Alcindor, Larry Bird, Wilt Chamberlain, Magic Johnson and Michael Jordan

93 Sophomore

94 Lew Alcindor, later known as Kareem Abdul-Jabbar. (We are sure there were other people born on that day but he was the most famous so we chose him.)

95 Pepperdine. Averitt scored an average of 33.9 points a game during the 1972-73 season.

Lew Alcindor

96 At what school did Kiki Vandeweghe play?

 97 What player was dominating the game to such an extent that the NCAA began disallowing the dunk in 1967?

 98 Who was named the Most Outstanding Player of the 1988 NCAA tournament?

 99 What position did Pete Maravich play at Louisiana State University?

 100 What team did Joe Barry Carroll play for in the 1980 Final Four?

 101 From what university is Toby Roybals the first player to have his number retired?

 102 At what university did Willis Reed play?

 103 What Virginia star established himself as the all-time Division I scoring leader from the state of Virginia?

 104 How many points did Bill Bradley score against Wichita State in the 1965 NCAA consolation game?

 105 Who led the 1979 national champion Michigan State team in scoring and rebounding?

 106 Name the only two players to become the National Player of the Year in their first varsity season.

 107 What university did Sean Elliott attend?

 108 For what SEC team did Bernard King play collegiate basketball?

 109 Where did one time SMU coach John Shumate play collegiately?

 110 At what Southwest Conference school did Ricky Pierce play?

96 The University of California-Los Angeles

97 Lew Alcindor, of UCLA

98 Danny Manning, of Kansas

99 Guard

100 Purdue

101 The University of New Mexico

102 Grambling

103 Bryant Stith

104 58 points

105 Gregory Kelser (I bet you thought it was Magic Johnson...)

106 Bill Walton of UCLA and Oscar Robertson of Cincinnati

107 University of Arizona

108 Tennessee

109 Notre Dame

110 Rice

Bill Walton

111 There have been two pairs of National Players of the Year that share the same last name. One is Bill and Cazzie. The other Glenn and David. What are their last names?

 112 Where did Elgin Baylor begin his collegiate career?

 113 What position did Gail Goodrich play at UCLA?

 114 In 1978, the Rupp Award for the *AP* Player of the Year went to which Marquette player?

 115 Former Kansas standout Rex Walters began his college career at what university?

 116 What UCLA player was named the MOP of the 1970 NCAA tournament?

 117 Roy Tarpley, Gary Grant, Glen Rice and Rumeal Robinson were all starters at what school?

 118 Reggie Theus played at what college?

 119 What is Bo Kimble's given first name?

 120 Who was the first Final Four player to be named Most Outstanding Player three straight years?

 121 What 6-foot 10-inch UCLA center was named the Most Outstanding Player of the 1975 NCAA tournament?

 122 What basketball team did Baskerville Holmes play for in the 1985 Final Four?

 123 Marvin Webster is the all-time leading scorer of what university?

 124 What 6-foot 5-inch Northeast Louisiana player averaged over 20 points and over 10 rebounds per game in each of his four seasons?

 125 Where did Michael Jordan play collegiately?

111 Bill and Cazzie Russell and Glenn and David Robinson

112 College of Idaho, in 1955. He later transferred to Seattle.

113 Guard

114 Butch Lee

115 Northwestern

116 Sidney Wicks

117 Michigan

118 University of Nevada-Las Vegas (UNLV)

119 Greg

120 Lew Alcindor, of UCLA

121 Rich Washington. He was the 1st round pick of the Kansas City Kings in the NBA draft.

122 Memphis State

123 Morgan State

124 Calvin Natt

125 North Carolina

Sidney Wicks

3-PT **126** Where did John Stockton play collegiately?

2-PT **127** At what university did Bob Cousy play?

3-PT **128** What 7-foot Western Kentucky player set an NCAA record by attempting 138 field goals in five games during the 1971 NCAA tournament?

2-PT **129** Steve Alford played at what university?

3-PT **130** Who was the only Final Four Most Outstanding Player who was not among the top five scorers on his team?

3-PT **131** Ernie DiGregorio played at what university?

3-PT **132** Who were the starting forwards for UCLA when they won the national championship over Memphis State in 1973?

3-PT **133** What Murray State player led the nation in rebounding in 1992 with an average of 14.4 rebounds per game?

2-PT **134** What player nicknamed Magic led Michigan State to the 1979 NCAA title?

3-PT **135** Who was the only player to score 20 or more points in a game in the 1985 Final Four?

3-PT **136** What Carolina university did Alex English attend?

2-PT **137** Who was the MOP of the NCAA tournament in 1972 and 1973 and the NBA Finals MVP in 1977?

3-PT **138** Who did Danny Manning surpass when he became the all-time leading scorer in Kansas University men's basketball history in 1987?

2-PT **139** Vernon Butler, Kevin Sinnett, John Clune and David Robinson are the all-time leading scorers at what school?

126 Gonzaga

127 Holy Cross

128 Jim McDaniels

129 Indiana

130 Marvin Huffman, of Indiana, in 1940

131 Providence

132 Keith Wilkes and Larry Farmer

133 Popeye Jones

134 Earvin Johnson

135 Reggie Williams, of Georgetown

136 South Carolina

137 Bill Walton

138 Clyde Lovelette

139 Navy

John Stockton

3-PT **140** Who became the all-time leading scorer at Boston College in 1989?

3-PT **141** Who was the first player to score more than 40 points in his first NCAA tournament game?

3-PT **142** What two Tennessee players shared SEC Player of the Year honors in 1977?

3-PT **143** What Arizona player made a three-point field goal in 38 consecutive games from 1987 through 1988?

2-PT **144** Who was the MOP of the NCAA tournament in 1971, when UCLA beat Villanova?

2-PT **145** Who was the NCAA tournament MOP in 1982 and the NBA Finals MVP in 1988?

2-PT **146** Where did Mark Macon play collegiately?

2-PT **147** Who became the all-time leading scorer at the University of Connecticut in 1992?

2-PT **148** At what school did Richard Dumas play?

2-PT **149** What 7-foot 1-inch LSU sophomore led the nation in rebounding in 1991?

2-PT **150** Keith Lee, Elliot Perry and Larry Finch are three of the all-time leading scorers at what university?

3-PT **151** Who was the first player to score 30 points in NCAA tournament semifinal and final games in the same season?

2-PT **152** Who was the first player to twice convert more than twelve free throws without a miss in the NCAA tournament?

3-PT **153** What Big Eight university did veteran NBA player Ed Nealy attend?

3-PT **154** Mel Counts was the leading scorer in the 1963 NCAA tournament. What school did he play for?

140 Dana Barros

141 Johnny O'Brien, of Seattle, scored 42 points in 1953.

142 Ernie Grunfeld and Bernard King

143 Steve Kerr

144 Howard Porter, of Villanova, who scored 25 points in the final.

145 James Worthy, of North Carolina University and the Los Angeles Lakers

146 Temple

147 Chris Smith

148 Oklahoma State

149 Shaquille O'Neal averaged 14.7 rebounds per game in 1991.

150 Memphis State

151 Clyde Lovellette, of Kansas, in 1952

152 Bill Bradley, of Princeton, in 1965

153 Kansas State

154 Oregon State

155 What 6-foot 4-inch Temple player led the nation in scoring with a 29.2 average in 1951?

 156 Who was the MOP of the NCAA tournament in 1959 and was the MVP of the NBA Finals in 1969?

 157 Who were the three future NBA players on Michigan State's 1979 NCAA title team?

 158 What former Kansas junior college basketball player was the MOP of the 1987 Final Four?

 159 Bill Anderson was this schools' first 1,000-point career scorer and its first 20-win coach. Name the school.

 160 Kyle Macy was a standout at Kentucky from 1978 to 1980 after transferring from what Big Ten school?

 161 Who was the Most Valuable Player in the Pac-10 in the 1990-91 season?

 162 What Seton Hall player became the Big East conference's all-time leading scorer during the 1992-93 season?

 163 NBA star Theodore Blue Edwards played basketball at what college?

 164 What Iowa State Cyclone became the school's all-time leading scorer in 1988?

 165 In what categories did Hank Gathers of Loyola Marymount lead the nation in 1989?

 166 Only two players have been named to the NCAA Final Four All-Time Team without winning a national championship. Who are they?

 167 The University of Alabama has only one player who has scored more than 2,000 points in the school's history. Name the player.

 168 Will Perdue played at what university?

155 Bill Mlkvy

156 Jerry West

157 Magic Johnson, Greg Kelser and Jay Vincent

158 Keith Smart, of Indiana

159 Lafayette

160 Purdue

161 Terrell Brandon, of the University of Oregon

162 Terry Dehere

163 East Carolina

164 Jeff Grayer, with 2,502 points

165 Scoring and rebounding

166 Larry Bird, of Indiana State, and Wilt Chamberlain, of Kansas

167 Reggie King, 1976-79, with 2,168 points

168 Vanderbilt

169 At what university did Gary Payton play?

 170 Glenn "Doc" Rivers played at what university?

 171 Who was the MOP of the 1992 NCAA tournament?

 172 What team did Dereck Whittenburg play for in the 1983 Final Four?

 173 Wendall Ladner, Clarence Weatherspoon and Tom Bishop were all outstanding players at what university?

 174 Rich Beard played at what university?

 175 Who was the first major college player to score more than 21,000 points in the NBA after never participating in either the NIT or NCAA tournament?

 176 Dominique Wilkins played at what university?

 177 Detlef Schrempf played at what university?

 178 What school did future NBA players Darrell Allums, Don Barksdale and Ralph Drollinger attend?

 179 What LSU player was the first pick of the 1992 NBA draft?

 180 What 6-foot 5-inch Connecticut player lead the nation in rebounding in 1954 and finished his career averaging more than 21 rebounds per game?

 181 Who was the first Texas Longhorn enshrined in the Basketball Hall of Fame?

182 At what university did JoJo White play?

169 Oregon State

170 Marquette

171 Bobby Hurley, of Duke

172 North Carolina State

173 Southern Mississippi

174 The University of Louisville

175 Robert Parish, of Centenary

176 Georgia

177 Washington

178 The University of California-Los Angeles

179 Shaquille O'Neal

180 Art Quimby averaged 22.6 rebounds per game in 1954 to lead the nation in that category. Ironically, he upped his average to 24.4 per game the following season but was edged out by Charlie Slack of Marshall, who averaged 25.6 rebounds per game.

181 Slater Martin

182 Kansas

3-PT **183** Who is the tallest player in Marist basketball history?

3-PT **184** What 6-foot 1-inch Bowling Green guard led the nation in scoring in 1964 with a 36.7 point average?

2-PT **185** At what Texas school was Nate Archibald a star from 1968 through 1970?

2-PT **186** What school did Cazzie Russell play for in the 1964 and 1965 Final Fours?

2-PT **187** What Princeton basketball player won the James E. Sullivan Award in 1965?

3-PT **188** Who was the first freshman in NCAA history to score over 900 points in a season?

2-PT **189** John Havlicek played at what university?

2-PT **190** What Ohio State basketball player was named *Sports Illustrated's* Sportsman of the Year in 1961?

2-PT **191** Name one of the first two players under 6-foot 4-inches to register over 2,000 career points and 1,000 career rebounds.

2-PT **192** What Duke star made a last-second shot in overtime to beat Kentucky in the 1992 East Regionals?

3-PT **193** In 1990, what player became the all-time leading scorer at the University of Texas?

2-PT **194** Where did 7-foot 4-inch NBA veteran Mark Eaton play collegiately?

2-PT **195** What player scored 31 points for Michigan in the 1989 championship game and was named the MOP?

2-PT **196** What player won Southwest Conference Player of the Decade honors for the 1980s?

183 Rik Smits at 7-foot 4-inches

184 Howard Komives

185 Texas-El Paso

186 Michigan

187 Bill Bradley

188 Chris Jackson, of Louisiana State

189 Ohio State

190 Jerry Lucas

191 Jerry West, of West Virginia, and Nick Werkman, of Seton Hall

192 Christian Laettner

193 Travis Mays, who scored 2,279 points in his career.

194 The University of California-Los Angeles (UCLA)

195 Glen Rice

196 Hakeem Olajuwon, of the University of Houston

CHAPTER 7
RECORDS

 1 Who holds the NCAA single game scoring record versus a Division I opponent?

 2 What team holds the NCAA record for most consecutive non-losing seasons?

 3 Who was the first player in NCAA history to have at least 400 assists in a single season?

 4 What LSU player set an NCAA record by making 30 free throws in a single game in 1969?

 5 Who set an NCAA record with 51 rebounds in a single game in 1953?

 6 Who was the first player in NCAA history to have 150 steals in a season?

 7 1953 through 1956 were undoubtedly the best years for players to average what?

 8 What team set an NCAA record with 28 losses in one season?

 9 What Big Eight team set an NCAA record in 1988 with 436 steals?

 10 During the 1996-1997 season, this team had the largest rebounding margin over its opponets at 10.9.

11 What team set an NCAA record by averaging 122.4 points per game in 1990?

12 What is the maximum number of regular-season games an NCAA Division I school can participate in?

 13 What is the length of a basketball court?

1 Kevin Bradshaw, of U.S. International, scored 72 points against Loyola (Cal.) on January 5, 1991.

2 Kentucky, with 60, from 1928 through 1988 (they did not play basketball during the 1953 season).

3 Mark Wade, of UNLV, in 1987

4 Pete Maravich attempted 31 free throws, making 30, versus Oregon State.

5 Bill Chambers, of William and Mary, rebounded the ball 51 times against Virginia, February 14, 1953.

6 Mookie Blaylock, of Oklahoma, in 1988

7 Rebounds. 15 out of the top 25 season rebounding average records were set in between 1953 and 1956.

8 Prairie View went 0-28 in 1992.

9 Oklahoma, led by Mookie Blaylock with 150 steals.

10 Utah State

11 Loyola Marymount, which scored over 100 points in a game 28 times in 1990 (another record).

12 Twenty-seven

13 94 feet

14 True or false: A player may legally rise or jump vertically and occupy the space within his or her vertical plane.

15 In the original rules of basketball, what did the ball have to do to count as a goal?

16 What rule change occurred in 1993 that decreased the number of possible turnovers in a game?

17 What is the only time a coach can leave the coaching box during a game?

18 What equipment change before the 1913-1914 season helped speed up the game of basketball?

19 To how many prospects can a Division I school provide paid-visits in one year? Is it 10, 12, or 15?

20 Does a missed shot by a player being fouled count as an attempted shot?

21 When is a player considered finished with the act of shooting?

22 What is the "charity stripe" also known as?

23 How many feet above the floor is the top of the backboard?

24 In the original rules of basketball, how long was a player disqualified after committing his second foul?

25 What is the length of an extra period?

26 What happens when players from both teams cause a free throw violation by breaking the plane of the free throw lane?

27 In the original rules of basketball, what would happen if a team committed three consecutive fouls (before the opposing team committed a foul)?

14 True (really!)

15 Go into the basket and stay there—only later were the bottoms of the baskets removed.

16 The elimination of the 5-second call when a player is dribbling. This rule was reinstated for the 1997-98 season.

17 When the coach seeks information from the scorer's table.

18 The bottom of the net was left open to allow the ball to pass through it.

19 Fifteen

20 No attempt on the goal is recorded.

21 When both feet have touched the ground.

22 The free throw line

23 13 feet

24 Until the next goal was made.

25 Five minutes

26 The ball becomes dead when a violation by the free thrower's team occurs, and the ball is awarded to the other team. If the non-shooting team commits the violation and the shooter misses, he or she is awarded another charity toss.

27 The opposing team would be awarded a goal.

28 What color must the rim be?

 29 How many seconds does a team have to move the ball from their backcourt to their frontcourt?

 30 How wide is the free throw lane?

 31 Can an eligible Division I player participate in a summer basketball league?

 32 What is the main difference in NCAA requirements between teams belonging to Division I and Division II?

 33 How long can an offensive player stay within the boundaries of the free throw lane?

 34 In 1949, coaches were first allowed to do what during a game?

 35 How many summer basketball leagues can a Division I player participate in and retain his eligilbility?

 36 How many contests can a Division I school play during a season against non-Division I schools and retain its Division I status?

 37 What was the distance of the three-point line during the Southern Conference's experiment with the three-point shot in 1980?

 38 The ball is touching the side of the rim and a player touches the net while jumping for the ball. Is basket interference called?

 39 How many fouls disqualify a player?

 40 At what distance is the three-point line in college?

 41 Who provides the ball for a basketball game?

28 Bright orange

29 Ten seconds from the time a player first touches the ball inbounds.

30 12 feet

31 Yes, provided he or she is the only player on the team with college eligibility.

32 The number of Division I opponents on their regular season schedule.

33 Three seconds. An offensive player must keep at least one foot outside the boundaries to avoid a violation.

34 Speak to players during a time out. We have to wonder if this rule change was welcomed by the players....

35 One

36 Four

37 The three-point line was measured at 21-feet 9-inches.

38 No, because the ball was not touching the top of the rim, nor was it inside the cylinder above the rim.

39 Five

40 It is 19 feet 9 inches from the center of the basket.

41 The home team

42 What is called when contact occurs between an offensive player and a defensive player inside the defensive player's vertical plane?

 43 What happens if a team adds a player to its squad after a game has begun?

 44 When is a player awarded a bonus free throw?

 45 Do unsporting or contact technical fouls count toward a player's five fouls for disqualification and toward team fouls for bonus free throw situations?

 46 Why was *The Triangle,* a magazine that the School for Christian Workers published on January 15, 1892 , an important printed material for college basketball?

 47 When was the 45-second clock introduced? Was it 1982, 1984, 1986, or 1988?

 48 Who decides which direction the teams will play in the first half of a college basketball game?

 49 In the original rules of basketball, what would occur if a game ended in a draw?

 50 How many leather panels are on a basketball?

 51 What happens if a player leaves a marked lane space after the ball is given to the free thrower?

 52 Are free throws awarded after a double personal foul?

 53 What is a turnover?

 54 Who is the only person on a team legally allowed to address an official on matters of interpretation?

 55 What happens if two of more players on the same team are wearing identical numbers?

42 Charging

43 A technical foul is assessed.

44 After his opponent has 7 team fouls and he converts the first free throw for a common foul, or after his opponent has 10 team fouls.

45 Yes

46 It was the first printing of Dr. James Naismith's *13 Original Rules of Basketball*.

47 1986

48 The visiting team

49 The captains could elect to continue the game until another goal is made.

50 Eight

51 A violation is called. If the free throw attempt is missed, another try is awarded to the free thrower.

52 No

53 The loss of possession without a goal attempt

54 The team captain

55 The second-listed player and any following player is assessed a technical foul.

56 Where is the base line on a basketball court?

 57 The accidental loss of player control by unintentionally dropping the basketball or permitting it to slip from one's grasp is the definition of what?

 58 How many expense-paid visits can a Division I basketball recruit have to different schools?

 59 When is a game officially over?

 60 Are points scored by a player with five fouls counted if the scorers do not notify the officials of the disqualification?

 61 How many expense-paid visits can a Division I basketball recruit have to the same school?

 62 What must be two inches in width and have a radius of two feet?

 63 In the original rules of basketball, what would occur if a player committed a foul with the intent to injure another player?

 64 In the original rules of basketball, how many steps could a player take before passing the ball?

 65 What is it called when an offensive player keeps both feet inside the free throw lane for more the three seconds?

 66 When is the shot clock reset?

56 The end boundary line beneath each basket

57 A fumble

58 Five

59 When the referee approves the final score.

60 Yes, the player is immediately removed from the game, but the points scored by the player are counted.

61 One

62 The center circle

63 The player was disqualified for the rest of the game, and no substitute was allowed.

64 None, the player had to throw it from the spot where he caught it.

65 A three-second violation and the ball is awarded to the opposite team behind the end line.

66 When control of the ball changes between teams, when the ball touches the rim after an attempted shot, or when a foul or violation occurs.

CHAPTER 8
TOURNAMENTS

3-PT **1** What school, with at least 15 games played, is the furthest below .500 in its NCAA tournament record?

3-PT **2** Who were the big four at the inaugural Big Four Classic at the Indianapolis Hoosier Dome on December 5, 1987?

3-PT **3** What is the only Pac-10 team to never reach the Final Four?

2-PT **4** Name the teams that participated in the 1991 Final Four played in the Hoosier Dome in Indianapolis?

3-PT **5** What was the University of Massachusetts record in the NCAA tournament during Julius Erving's years on the team?

2-PT **6** What was the first year two teams from the same conference played in the NCAA tournament? Was it 1944, 1954, 1974, or 1984?

2-PT **7** What region in the NCAA tournament has produced the most champions?

3-PT **8** What four teams played in the 1988 Final Four?

2-PT **9** What team won ten national titles in twelve years, from 1964 through 1975?

2-PT **10** In what year did the NCAA first use a Saturday afternoon, Monday evening format for the Final Four? Was it 1973, 1975, or 1977?

2-PT **11** What two schools have had at least four different coaches take it into the NCAA tournament, with all four coaches having winning tournament records?

3-PT **12** Name four players from the NCAA tournament All-Decade Team of the 1950s.

1 Miami University (Ohio), with a record of 3-15

2 Kentucky, Indiana, Notre Dame and Louisville

3 Arizona State

4 Kansas, North Carolina, UNLV and Duke

5 Massachusetts did not participate in the tournament during Erving's two seasons on the team.

6 Nineteen forty-four, when Missouri played Iowa State and both were from the Big Six Conference. Iowa State was substituted for Arkansas because the Arkansas team had a bus accident on the way to the tournament in Kansas City. Several team members were injured and unable to continue play.

7 The West or Far West, with 18 as of 1997

8 Kansas, Oklahoma, Arizona and Duke

9 UCLA

10 1973

11 Kentucky and Kansas

12 Elgin Baylor, Wilt Chamberlain, Clyde Lovellette, Tom Gola, K.C. Jones, Oscar Robertson, Guy Rodgers, Len Rosenbluth and Jerry West

13 What was the first team to be invited to play in both the NIT and NCAA tournament in the same season?

 14 What team holds the record of most consecutive tournament appearances?

 15 In 1970, these four teams arrived at the Final Four with the highest combined winning percentage ever - .945 - 103 wins and six losses. Name them.

 16 What team did Texas Western need two overtimes to defeat on their way to the national championship in 1966?

 17 What two teams in the 1984 Final Four did not compete in the championship game?

 18 In the last thirty-four years, what is the only national champion to enter the NCAA tournament with less than twenty victories?

 19 What was the first team to capture three NCAA championships?

 20 Who was the lowest-seeded school to defeat a number one-seeded school in the NCAA tournament?

 21 From 1964 through 1979, the UCLA Bruins won ten NCAA titles and finished second how many times?

 22 What school beat second-ranked DePaul 82-75 in the opening round of the 1982 NCAA tournament?

 23 In UCLA's run of seven consecutive championships from 1967 through 1973, what was their smallest margin of victory in the title game?

 24 What ACC team won the NIT in 1992?

25 What team has won the most NCAA championship games without a championship game loss?

13 Duquesne University, in 1940

14 North Carolina

15 UCLA   26-2
New Mexico State   26-2
Jacksonville   26-1
Saint Bonaventure 25-1

16 Kansas

17 Kentucky and Virginia

18 Villanova, in 1985

19 Kentucky

20 Number 11 seed   Louisiana State University defeated number 1 seed Kentucky in 1986.

21 Zero

22 Boston College

23 Five, against Florida State in 1972

24 Virginia beat Notre Dame 81-76 in overtime.

25 Indiana University is 5-0.

2-PT **26** Beginning in 1964, the UCLA Bruins won the NCAA championship nine times in a ten-year period. What school won it the other year?

3-PT **27** What four teams played in the 1987 Final Four in New Orleans?

3-PT **28** What conference's teams were beaten in the 1985 regional finals by the Big East's three eventual Final Four representatives?

3-PT **29** What Illinois university hosted the NCAA championship game in 1939 and 1956?

2-PT **30** What was the first school to lose three national championship games in a city where it enjoyed a distinct home-crowd advantage?

2-PT **31** What team vacated their NCAA tournament games from 1980 to 1982?

3-PT **32** Who was the leading scorer for Texas Western, with 20 points, when the Miners upset Kentucky in the 1966 NCAA title game?

3-PT **33** What school did MVP Randolph Keys lead past La Salle 84-80 for the NIT championship on March 26, 1987?

2-PT **34** What team has won the NCAA championship, although from a school not located in one of the forty-eight contiguous United States?

2-PT **35** In what year did the NCAA tournament field expand from 16 to 32 teams? Was it 1972, 1973, 1974, or 1975?

3-PT **36** What four teams participated in the 1981 Final Four in Philadelphia?

2-PT **37** What was the first school to win three consecutive national championships?

26 Texas Western (now UTEP) beat Kentucky in the 1966 finals.

27 Nevada-Las Vegas, Indiana, Providence and Syracuse

28 The Atlantic Coast Conference

29 Northwestern

30 Kansas lost title games in 1940, 1953, and 1957 in Kansas City, Missouri, a mere 40 miles from its campus.

31 Oregon State

32 Bobby Joe Hill

33 Southern Mississippi

34 Georgetown, which is in the District of Columbia.

35 1975

36 Louisiana State, Indiana, North Carolina and Virginia. Indiana defeated North Carolina, 63-50, to win the national championship.

37 UCLA in 1967, 1968 and 1969

38 What was the first team that had to win six games in the NCAA tournament to become the national champion?

 39 In what year did the NCAA first supervise the NCAA tournament?

 40 What team had an NCAA tournament record of 21-2 from 1989 to 1992?

 41 What was the first team to have at least one player score in double digits in the national championship game?

 42 What was the first school to have three players score more than 20 points each in a Final Four game?

 43 What three schools from the state of Kansas have gone to the Final Four?

 44 Which school has made the most trips to the NIT?

 45 What place in the ACC did North Carolina State finish the season before going on to win the national championship in 1983?

 46 What three teams from California won the national championship before UCLA?

 47 Name five players from the NCAA tournament All-Decade Team of the 1980s.

 48 Who are the five members of the Big 10 Conference to have won national championships?

 49 What national championship team's lineup averaged eighteen years of age?

50 Who was the NCAA Tournament's Most Outstanding Player in both 1984 and 1985?

38 North Carolina State, in 1983

39 1940 (The first NCAA tournament, in 1939, was supervised by the National Association of Basketball Coaches.)

40 Duke

41 Georgetown, in 1943

42 Memphis State's Larry Kenon, Ronnie Robinson, and Larry Finch, in the 1973 national semifinals

43 Kansas, Kansas State and Wichita State

44 St. John's

45 Fourth

46 Stanford, in 1942, San Francisco, in 1955 and 1956, and California, in 1959

47 Steve Alford, Johnny Dawkins, Patrick Ewing, Darrell Griffith, Michael Jordan, Rodney McCray, Akeem Olajuwon, Ed Pinckney, Isiah Thomas and James Worthy

48 Michigan, Indiana, Michigan State, Ohio State and Wisconsin

49 Utah, in 1944

50 Patrick Ewing, of Georgetown

3-PT 51 In what Final Four was the first All-Tournament Team selected by the sports writers?

2-PT 52 How many NCAA titles did Duke win during Danny Ferry's career with the Blue Devils?

3-PT 53 Who were the starting guards on Ohio State's 1960 national championship team?

2-PT 54 What Pac-10 team defeated Oklahoma 78-72 on March 29, 1991 to win the NIT championship?

3-PT 55 What is the first school to finish in the *AP* top 10 at least five times yet never make it to the Final Four?

3-PT 56 What was the first school to lose as many as twelve games in the opening round of the NCAA tournament?

3-PT 57 What was the first team to play only its starters in the national championship game?

3-PT 58 Who is the only team to reach the Final Four despite compiling a losing record in its conference and losing in the first round of its conference tournament?

3-PT 59 Who was the first player to lead an NCAA championship game in scoring while playing for his father?

2-PT 60 In 1974, Maryland finished their season 23-5, were 9-3 in the ACC, and were ranked fourth in the final *AP* poll. Why did they not play in the NCAA tournament?

2-PT 61 What four teams participated in the 1993 Final Four in New Orleans?

3-PT 62 What six teams have repeated as champions since the inception of the NCAA tournament?

51 The year was 1952 and Kansas center Clyde Lovellette was named to the team and named Most Outstanding Player after leading the Jayhawks to the national championship. Other players named to the team were Dean Kelley (Kansas), John Kerr (Illinois), Ron Macgilvray (St. John's) and Bob Zawoluk (St. John's).

52 None, despite going to the Final Four three times.

53 Larry Siegfried and Mel Nowell

54 Stanford

55 Maryland

56 Princeton

57 Loyola of Chicago, in 1963

58 Virginia had a 6-8 record in the ACC in 1984 and lost it's first conference tournament game.

59 Center Bob Allen, of Kansas, who played for his father, Phog Allen, in the 1940 title game.

60 They lost in the ACC tournament when only the conference tournament champion advanced. Eventual national champion N.C. State defeated Maryland 103-100 in overtime in the tournament final.

61 Kansas, Kentucky, Michigan and North Carolina

62 Oklahoma A & M, Kentucky, San Francisco, Cincinnati, UCLA and Duke

63 How many NCAA titles has Oregon won since the first, in 1939?

 64 Who were the Final Four teams in the 1992 NCAA tournament?

 65 Which is the only team from the old Big Eight Conference to never win an NCAA tournament game?

 66 What team did Bill Walton score his record 44 points against in an NCAA championship game?

 67 What two schools have won two NCAA championship games by only one point?

 68 This team lead the 1992 title game at halftime but lost by 20 points.

 69 What was the first year that the tournament was expanded to 64 teams? Was it 1983, 1985, or 1987?

 70 In what year was a second conference team other than the champion allowed to be selected as an at-large entry in the NCAA tournament?

 71 What school won four games by 2 points or less on its way to the national championship in 1983?

 72 Name four of the starting five for North Carolina's 1982 national championship team.

 73 What four teams participated in the 1982 Final Four in New Orleans?

 74 What was the first school to win back-to-back NCAA championships?

75 What is the first school with at least ten NCAA tournament losses that has never lost an opening round tournament game?

 76 What historically black college was the first such school to play in the National Invitational Tournament?

63 Zero

64 Michigan, Cincinnati, Duke and Indiana

65 Nebraska

66 Memphis State, in 1973

67 North Carolina, in 1957 and 1982 and Indiana in 1953 and 1987. Carolina beat Kansas in 1957 by one in three overtimes and Georgetown in 1982, 63-62. Indiana also defeated Kansas by one in 1953 and Syracuse by that narrowest of margins in 1987.

68 Michigan led at the half but lost to Duke.

69 1985

70 1975

71 North Carolina State

72 Matt Doherty, James Worthy, Sam Perkins, Jimmy Black and Michael Jordan

73 North Carolina, Houston, Louisville and Georgetown. North Carolina edged Georgetown, 63-62, to win the national championship.

74 Oklahoma A&M (now Oklahoma State) defeated New York University 49 - 45 in 1945 and North Carolina 43 - 40 in 1946.

75 Maryland

76 The University of Maryland-Eastern Shore, in 1974

3-PT **77** Name the four teams in the 1990 Final Four in Denver.

3-PT **78** How many of the top 10 seasonal scoring average leaders have taken their teams to the NCAA Tournament?

2-PT **79** What school from the SEC beat Seattle to win the 1958 NCAA title?

3-PT **80** Who is the only first-time entrant in the NCAA tournament to be seeded better than fifth, since the field expanded to forty-eight teams in 1980?

2-PT **81** Which Big Eight school was the first to win the NIT?

3-PT **82** Name three of the "Fabulous Five" starters on the 1947-48 Kentucky Wildcats.

2-PT **83** What Notre Dame star scored an NCAA-record 61 points against Ohio in a 1970 NCAA tournament game?

3-PT **84** On March 19, 1954, MVP Togo Palazzi led what school to a 71-62 victory over Duquesne to win the NIT?

1-PT **85** What is the only conference that has five different members who have been national champions?

3-PT **86** What team was the first to win the NIT and the NCAA championships in the same season?

3-PT **87** Name four players from the NCAA tournament All-Decade Team of the 1970s.

3-PT **88** Who was the first team to enter the NCAA tournament with a losing record and win a game?

2-PT **89** What two teams in the 1982 Final Four did not compete in the championship game?

2-PT **90** Which school has won the most NIT championships?

77 Georgia Tech, Arkansas, Duke and Nevada-Las Vegas

78 Only one, Austin Carr of Notre Dame. His 1970 average is ninth and his 1971 average is tenth in seasonal scoring average.

79 Kentucky by a score of 84 - 72

80 Georgia

81 Colorado, in 1940

82 Alex Groza, Ralph Beard, Kenny Rollins, Wah Wah Jones and Cliff Barker

83 Austin Carr

84 Holy Cross

85 The Big 10

86 City College of New York in the 1949-1950 season. They defeated Bradley in both games.

87 Kent Benson, Larry Bird, Jack Givens, Earvin Johnson, Marques Johnson, Scott May, David Thompson, Bill Walton, Sidney Wicks and Keith Wilkes

88 Bradley won two games in the 1955 tournament after compiling a regular season record of 7-19.

89 Houston and Louisville

90 St. John's

91 What four teams from the state of Indiana have been to the Final Four?

 92 Who was the first Final Four team to have three players average more than 20 points per game in the same season?

 93 What school has lost two NCAA championship games by only one point?

 94 What team won the very first NCAA tournament game?

 95 What was the first conference to have three of its member teams advance to the Final Four in the same year?

 96 What was the first school to win NCAA, NIT and NAIA championships?

 97 What school was the first to be ranked number one entering back-to-back tournaments only to lose opening round games each year?

 98 Who is the only team from the Big East Conference to never win an NCAA tournament game?

 99 Who was the first double-digit seeded team to reach the Final Four?

 100 Who did North Carolina State defeat to win the NCAA title in 1983?

 101 Who was the first school to lead the nation in scoring offense and win the NCAA title in the same season?

 102 What is the only conference whose members have all participated in at least ten NCAA tournament games?

 103 What team reached the Final Four six times in seven years, from 1986 through 1992?

104 What is the only team to lose in both the NIT and NCAA championship games in the same year?

91 Indiana, Indiana State, Notre Dame and Purdue

92 Georgia Tech was led by Dennis Scott, Brian Oliver and Kenny Anderson in 1990.

93 Kansas, in 1953 to Indiana and in 1957 to North Carolina

94 Villanova defeated Brown, 42-30, on March 17, 1939, in Philadelphia, Pennsylvania.

95 The Big East, in 1985, was represented by Georgetown, St. John's and Villanova.

96 Louisville

97 DePaul lost to UCLA in 1980 and to St. Joseph's in 1981.

98 The University of Miami (Florida)

99 In 1986, Louisiana State University was seeded eleventh and advanced to the Final Four.

100 Houston

101 Ohio State, in 1960

102 The Atlantic Coast Conference

103 Duke

104 Bradley lost to C.C.N.Y. in both the NCAA and NIT finals in 1950.

3-PT **105** Name two players from the NCAA tournament All-Decade Team of the 1940s.

3-PT **106** What school shot an NCAA title game record 78.6 percent from the floor in 1985 in defeating the nation's top-ranked team to win the title?

2-PT **107** Who is the only team from the Big 10 Conference to never win an NCAA tournament game?

3-PT **108** What was the first team to have twenty-six different players appear in its games during a season and win an NCAA title?

2-PT **109** What two teams were undefeated going into the Final Four in 1976?

2-PT **110** Name the only two teams in the 1980s to win two NCAA championships.

2-PT **111** What team, known mainly for winning NCAA championships, won the NIT championship in 1985?

2-PT **112** In 1971, the University of Southern California finished their season 24-2, were 12-2 in the Pac 10, and were ranked fifth in the final *AP* poll. Why did they not play in the NCAA tournament?

3-PT **113** What UCLA player was named the Most Outstanding Player of the 1964 NCAA Tournament? (Clue: He later coached at his alma mater).

2-PT **114** In 1988, two teams from what conference met in the NCAA championship game which was played at Kemper Arena in Kansas City, Missouri?

2-PT **115** How many times have two teams from the same state played each other in an NCAA championship game?

3-PT **116** In what year was the first National Invitational Tournament held?

105 Ralph Beard, Howie Dallmar, Dwight Eddleman, Arnie Ferrin, Alex Groza, George Kaftan, Bob Kurland, Jim Pollard, Ken Sailors and Gerald Tucker

106 Villanova defeated top-ranked Georgetown.

107 Northwestern

108 Oklahoma State, in 1946

109 Indiana, at 30-0, and Rutgers, at 31-0

110 Louisville and Indiana

111 The UCLA Bruins

112 Only the conference champion advanced and both their losses were to UCLA.

113 Walt Hazzard

114 The Big Eight Conference (Kansas and Oklahoma). It marked the 50th anniversary of the NCAA Tournament.

115 Twice: Cincinnati defeated Ohio State in 1961 and 1962.

116 The first NIT was played in 1938, one year before the first NCAA Tournament was played.

117 What school did Kansas beat in the 1988 Midwest Regional Final after losing to them twice earlier in the same season?

 118 How many Final Four appearances have the Fighting Irish had?

 119 How many national championships did Georgetown win while Patrick Ewing was on the team?

 120 Who is the only school to have six different coaches compile losing NCAA tournament records?

 121 What team did Arizona defeat to win the 1997 NCAA title?

 122 How many NCAA tournament appearances did Minnesota make while Kevin McHale was on its team?

 123 What is the only school to appear in as many as eight consecutive NCAA tournaments starting with its first appearance in the tournament?

 124 What team vacated their NCAA tournament games from 1971 to 1973?

 125 On March 14, 1981, in the NCAA Midwest Regional, who launched a desperation 49-footer with 1 second left, upsetting the defending champion Louisville Cardinals?

 126 What two Big Eight teams have never reached the Final Four?

 127 What school has had twelve top 10 finishes in the final *AP* poll yet has a losing record in the NCAA tournament?

 128 What team vacated their NCAA tournament games from 1982 to 1986?

 129 In 1982, Georgetown's Fred Brown threw a misguided pass to what North Carolina player at the end of the NCAA title game?

117 Kansas State

118 One, in 1978

119 One, in 1984 when Georgetown defeated Houston 84 -75.

120 Miami University (Ohio) is 3-15 under six different coaches.

121 Kentucky, which failed to defend its national championship from the previous season.

122 They did not make it to the tournament during his college career.

123 Idaho State participated in the tournament for the first time in 1953, a run which would extend to eight consecutive years.

124 Long Beach State

125 U. S. Reed, of the University of Arkansas

126 Nebraska and Missouri

127 Notre Dame

128 Memphis State

129 James Worthy

UPC

7 08850 11062 6

00995